A Simple Guide

ELEMENTS OF THE TABLE

for Hosts and Guests

LYNN ROSEN

PHOTOGRAPHS BY WALTER ROSEN
AND PATRICK SNOOK

CLARKSON POTTER/PUBLISHERS
NEW YORK

Published in the United States by Clarkson Potter/Publishers,
an imprint of the Crown Publishing Group,
a division of Random House, Inc., New York.
www.crownpublishing.com
www.clarksonpotter.com

Clarkson N. Potter is a trademark and Potter and colophon are
registered trademarks of Random House, Inc.

Library of Congress Cataloging-in-Publication Data
is available on request.

ISBN 978-0-307-33933-1
Printed in Singapore

Design by Laura Palese and Danielle Deschenes

10   9   8   7   6   5   4   3   2

First Edition

CONTENTS

INTRODUCTION

Why Your Table Matters

Your dinner table is a place for celebrations, where you invite your guests to sit in comfort and partake of good food and conversation. The dinner table can be daunting, however, with its complicated array of dishes, utensils, and serving pieces, and its mystifying rules regarding behavior. It is one thing to possess a collection of elegant tableware; it is quite another to know how to put it to proper use. And, as every host or hostess quickly learns, one of the foundations of a successful dinner party is a well-set, inviting table.

When I was a girl, one of my tasks at home was to set the table for dinner. This was an especially important job whenever my mother entertained guests. We brought out all the fine china, the silver, and the crystal, and I had to be sure to put everything in *exactly* the right place–not one inch to the right or left of where it was supposed to be. I was certain my mother made up all these table-setting rules simply to torture me. But when I began to study dining history and traditions, I learned that what she had taught me was only part of a wealth of dinner-table rules that are the result of centuries of changing customs and technological improvements.

Table manners evolved for a purpose, to enable a group of people to sit together at a dining table in a civilized way and enjoy a meal without spilling food all over themselves or one another, breaking dishes, or accidentally sticking each other with a fork or a knife. "Prevention of the violence which could so easily break out at table is . . . one of the principal aims of table manners," notes dining expert Margaret Visser in her classic book *The Rituals of Dinner.* There was a time when people really did need to worry about their personal safety when sitting with strangers at a table filled with pointy utensils! Today, table manners provide a set of reliable rules that allow us to dine in comfort, knowing that the meal will be pleasant and the dinner guests, even those we've never met before, will behave.

This book is designed to make sure you know the rules of the table and that you don't embarrass yourself. For hosts and hostesses, it provides a simple step-by-step guide to setting the table and serving food, guaranteed to facilitate stress-free dinner parties! The decorative elements of the table, such as napkin folding and formal service, are illustrated. Easy instructions on how to use everything properly help both guests and hosts avoid gaffes. *Elements of the Table* also gives you a taste of the history behind our contemporary dining customs and table etiquette. That way, once you've impressed your guests with the beauty of your table, you'll have something new and interesting to chat about over dinner!

What's on the Table?

Your tableware is divided into three main categories: china, silver, and crystal. In each of these categories, there are place pieces, which are used at individual place settings, and service pieces, which are used to contain and serve food (seems obvious enough!).

PLACE SETTINGS

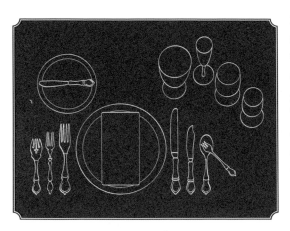

Imagine each place setting, also referred to as a "cover," as a rectangle, with the dinner or service plate in the center. Utensils should have about half an inch of space between them, and the bottom of each utensil and the plate should be set approximately an inch from the edge of the table. Each cover should be 18 to 20 inches from the next, to provide elbow room for the dinner guests and enough space for the servers to fit in between and do their job.

Each setting will contain elements from the three categories of tableware:

- China: a dinner or service plate, a soup bowl, and perhaps a bread and butter plate.

- Silverware: a selection of forks, knives, and spoons as dictated by the menu (it is permissible to eat some foods with your fingers–see page 76–but not many!)

- Crystal: wineglasses, a water goblet, and perhaps a champagne glass

The place setting will be finished with a cloth napkin.

A place setting is in some ways like a puzzle: each piece set before the diner corresponds to a dish or a course being served at the meal. Just by looking at a place setting a knowledgeable guest can discern something of what will be served at the meal to come. Soupspoon and soup bowl in place? Then soup is to be served, of course. In the same way, salad fork = salad, and fish fork = fish–providing, of course, that the diner can identify a fish fork (a quick hint: check out page 62)!

SERVING PIECES

Various serving pieces meant to be shared by all are placed in central locations on the table or sideboard. These include all manner of plates, bowls, and other containers, each with a utensil for serving. Some pieces may be in place before the start of the meal, and others are brought in and taken out during service. Table linen, referred to as napery, and table decor–perhaps a centerpiece or a candelabra–will also adorn the table.

EVERYTHING IN ITS PLACE—OR NOT!

Each piece of tableware is designed for a specific function, but you can be flexible about how you use your dinnerware to meet the needs of your service. If you don't have a dessert plate, substitute a salad plate. Use a salad fork in place of a fish fork. Use that odd little fork with a wide head and shortened tines, originally made as a sardine fork, on your cheese tray. Know the proper use of each item–but don't be afraid to be creative!

CHAPTER 1

NAPERY

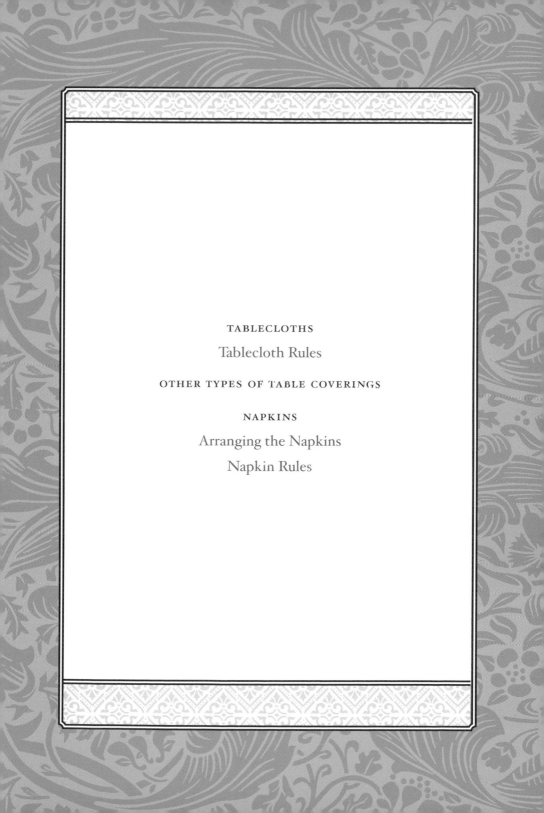

Much of the splendor of the dinner table is achieved through the use of beautiful napery. Although you might occasionally see a formal table set without a tablecloth to highlight the gleaming, highly polished wood, the dinner table is typically covered with a cloth, and each place setting includes a cloth napkin. From traditional white or ivory to a fabric with more color, pattern, or texture, your choice of napery provides a unifying element that makes your table look complete.

*T*ABLECLOTHS

Tablecloths have long been used as table accessories. The Romans found them to be very useful–as napkins. In feudal society, a tablecloth denoted rank, and only the nobility sat at covered tables. To cope with messy medieval meals, cloths were layered and removed as they became dirty. The Victorians employed this layering concept as well: "accidental cloths" were placed over certain areas of the table and removed after each course as necessary, so that dessert was often served on a bare tabletop.

Modern napery is available in an array of fabrics, from fine linens to easy-care synthetics, and comes in a range of colors and patterns. Select a style to match your tableware or the decor of your room, but to achieve the most elegant effect, keep it simple. The finer the cloth, the finer the table. Damask has always been the most formal and traditional choice of tablecloth, although it is also the most expensive and requires more care. Made with silk, linen, and other natural fibers, it has a reversible pattern woven into it. (See page 14 for an example of a damask weave, which originated in Damascus, Syria. Manufactured by SFERRA Fine Linens, all of the table linens featured in this book are examples of fine jacquard weaves, of which damask is one type.)

TABLECLOTH RULES

The tablecloth is the first thing to be placed on the table. Use a clean, pressed cloth, and center it over the table. The cloth should hang evenly around the table, falling 12 to 15 inches down from the edge of the table. (Luncheon cloths hang only a few inches over the edge of the table; buffet cloths fall to the floor.) You may wish to place pads under the cloth to further protect the table.

Because of the necessity of storing your cloth folded, it will likely have a crease no matter how much you press it. If the cloth has a crease, make sure the crease (or creases) runs straight down the table. In the seventeenth and eighteenth centuries, creases were fashionable and were purposely ironed in, and cloth napkins were stored in napkin presses to maintain crisp creases. When creases went out of fashion in the late nineteenth century, cloths were stored wrapped around tubes to keep them smooth.

TABLE TALK: DOILIES

In the late seventeenth century, according to author Louise Conway Belden, many Londoners purchased fabric from the shop of a draper named D'Oyley. Among his wares were "small napkins hostesses offered their guests for wiping their fingers after their large napkins had been removed." And thus the doily was born! Today, the doily is used not as a napkin but as a plate liner or to protect a bare table during the dessert course.

OTHER TYPES OF TABLE COVERINGS

After World War II, when the vast army of workers who once staffed the great English estates left for factory jobs and there were fewer staff to do the laundry and ironing, place mats became a simpler option than tablecloths. Place mats are rarely used for formal dining, however: they are too casual and break up the space on the table, leaving less usable surface area.

Table runners placed down each side of the table can be used instead of place mats or tablecloths (a mat is needed for the seats at the head and the foot of the table). Using a table runner over a tablecloth creates a very dressy effect for a formal table.

NAPKINS

In the sixteenth century, napkins came into common usage (before that a hand or a slab of bread might have been called into use!). Napkin rings were popular as well, but not as the decorative accessories they are today. Since laundry was not done with any great regularity, cloth napkins would be used for multiple meals between washings. An identifiable napkin ring ensured that the diner would at least be using his or her own dirty linen!

At first, napkins were worn over the shoulder or the arm, or even bib-style, attached to one's waistcoat with a silver napkin hook. As time went by, diners began to place their napkins in their laps. In the seventeenth century, as ladies' skirts grew more voluminous, napkins grew as well, to a size of 35 by 45 inches.

Once fork use became more common (see page 58) and made us neater eaters, napkins shrank in size. Today's typical dinner napkin is between 22 and 26 inches square. A luncheon napkin is smaller, from 14 to 18 inches square. There are also tea napkins (12 inches square) and cocktail napkins (4 to 6 inches square), although the latter are frequently made out of paper.

Fashion often had an influence on table customs. For example, the wide white starched and pleated collars worn by Elizabethan men made it hard for them to follow the custom of tying the napkin ends around their necks. Thus was born the phrase "making ends meet."

ARRANGING THE NAPKINS

There are many ways to arrange a napkin in a place setting. The most traditional approach at a formal table is to first fold the napkin in half and then in three folds into a neat rectangle, and place it on the service or dinner plate. This presentation not only takes up less space on a crowded table but also provides an obvious hint to the diner that he won't be able to get at his plate unless he puts his napkin on his lap! Another option is to roll the napkin, enclose it in a decorative napkin ring, and place it across the service or dinner plate. However, if the first course will be in place on the table when the guests are seated, lay the napkin on the table to the left of the forks.

Many hosts enjoy decorating their tables with intricately folded napkins. The design possibilities are endless, from the simple and traditional bishop's mitre to the elaborate lily fold. Folded napkins are then placed on the dinner or service plate, or occasionally in the water goblet. See page 101 for more on napkin folding, including examples and instructions for a range of decorative folds.

NAPKIN RULES

In the nineteenth century, the French had very exacting rules about napkin usage: for example, the person of highest rank at the table should unfold his napkin first, and one must never use a napkin to wipe one's nose. Today's napkin rules are equally rigid: Upon sitting down at the table, your first assignment is to place the napkin on your lap. At a small formal dinner, wait for the hostess to pick up her napkin, and then follow suit. Blowing your nose into a napkin is still quite inappropriate, and do try to blot your lipstick before dinner, so as not to leave your napkin bathed in Rampage Red.

If you leave your seat temporarily during the meal, place your napkin on your chair, not to the left of the plate as some diners insist. The etiquette experts I have consulted on this topic vote in favor of placing it on the chair! When leaving the table at the end of the meal, however, do place your napkin to the left side of the plate. Don't refold it; just pick it up by the center, gather the folds together, and lay it on the table. When the hostess places her napkin to the left of her plate, this signals the end of the meal.

Given the efficiency of modern washers and dryers, washing napkins after each use is the more common practice these days, but one woman told me that while staying at a European hotel she was asked at the end of a meal to write her name on an envelope and to place her napkin in it. Her napkin would be reused for the duration of her stay! It is interesting to note that the old way lives on in some places.

TABLE TEST

Q: TRUE OR FALSE: Always unfold your napkin on your lap.

A: FALSE. A large dinner napkin should be kept folded in half on your lap, with the opening to the front. A luncheon napkin can be fully opened on your lap.

CHAPTER 2

CHINA

THE BASIC CHINA PLACE SETTING

TYPES OF PLACE CHINA

Plates
- *Service Plate*
- *Dinner Plate*
- *Salad Plate*
- *Bread and Butter Plate*
- *Dessert Plate*
- *Other Types of Plates*

Bowls
- *Soup Bowl*
  - SOUP BOWL RULES
- *Fruit Bowl*

Cups
- *Coffee Cup*
  - COFFEE CUP RULES
- *Teacup*
  - TEACUP RULES

CHINA SERVING PIECES

Soup Tureen
  Soup Tureen Rules
Covered Vegetable Dish
Vegetable Dish
Oval Serving Platter
Gravy Boat
Salad Bowl
Bread Tray

Butter Dish
Salt and Pepper Shakers
Cake Plate
Coffeepot
Teapot
Sugar Bowl
Creamer
Other Serving Pieces

Chances are your china didn't come from China. But as early as the ninth century, the Chinese were the only ones who possessed the coveted secret formula for the most desired, top-of-the-line dinnerware: hard-paste porcelain. This is why your dinnerware is usually referred to as china. Today, many manufacturers, European, Asian, and American, make a variety of types and styles of china: from English bone china such as Spode and Wedgwood, and American bone china such as that made by Lenox, to European hard-paste porcelain–Bernardaud or Herend are examples. And while you probably use other types of pottery, such as earthenware or more casual stoneware, for everyday dining, your fancy china is likely to be porcelain.

The Basic China Place Setting

A standard place setting for fine china today usually includes five pieces: a dinner plate, a salad or dessert plate, a bread and butter plate, a cup, and a saucer. A more casual place setting likely includes a soup/cereal bowl in place of the bread and butter plate, and might have a mug rather than a cup and a saucer.

The five-piece place setting simplifies the process of acquiring china, because manufacturers provide all the pieces they think you will need. Some china, particularly European china, is also available for purchase by the piece. A typical collection includes the following pieces:

- Plates: service, dinner, salad, dessert, bread and butter

- Bowls: rim soup, coupe soup, fruit, cereal

- Cups and saucers: teacup and saucer, after-dinner coffee cup and saucer, breakfast cup and saucer, espresso or demitasse cup and saucer

AN AMERICAN IN LIMOGES

In the mid–nineteenth century, an American importer of European ceramics named David Haviland was taken by the beauty of a French porcelain cup shown to him by a customer. He went to the Limoges region of France, the source of this beautiful hard-paste porcelain, toured the factories, and began importing French porcelain. Soon he moved to Limoges, where in 1847 he and his brother Daniel opened their own decorating studio, followed by a factory in 1864. Haviland's wares were so successful in America that he ushered in the golden era of Limoges porcelain manufacture, from the mid–nineteenth century to about 1930. Limoges made during this period is treasured by collectors today.

The Haviland company is still a leader in the manufacture of Limoges porcelain. The photographs in this book feature their porcelain.

The open-stock method of acquiring china allows you to choose the pieces most suited to your style of entertaining, an option that may appeal to a more experienced host or hostess. Open stock also allows you to be creative and to mix and match patterns of place china. Matching tableware makes for an elegant and unified table setting, but there is a long-standing and quite proper tradition of mixing china patterns and styles. When done effectively, this style can make for a very dramatic table setting (see page 116).

Bridal registries, such as the one at Bloomingdale's, recommend what they think is a good number of place settings with which to start when first purchasing china: twelve of each of the pieces in a five-piece setting plus twelve rim soup bowls. Chargers–service plates–and other styles of bowls are also options (see page 31 for more on types of bowls).

TYPES OF PLACE CHINA

PLATES

If you were sitting down to dinner in medieval times, you would eat your meal from a trencher, a thick, often stale slice of bread with the crusts pared off. Although you could in theory eat your plate at the end of the meal, it was more common to collect the used trenchers and give them to the poor.

Trenchers were succeeded by wooden plates (or metal plates for the wealthy), and, with the growth of the ceramics industry in the seventeenth century, the adoption of ceramic dishes. Gradually the custom of using individual ceramic plates for each diner replaced the tradition of eating from individual trenchers or from communal bowls, and the use of the dinner plate became common by the nineteenth century. Over time, the dinner plate itself evolved into a variety of plates of different sizes.

 SERVICE PLATE

The service plate, also called a charger, is between 11 and 14 inches in diameter. It is placed in the center of the place setting and is on the table when diners are seated. Food is never placed directly on the service plate and the guest never moves the service plate (or any plate, for that matter–guests should always leave plates wherever their host or server has placed them).

If soup is to be served, the soup bowl (sometimes with an underliner) is placed on top of the service plate. If an appetizer is served, this plate is also placed on top of the service plate. Service plates may either match the main service china or have a complementary pattern or design. Some are made out of a different material, such as silver, pewter, or brass.

When the appetizer course is finished, the service plate is removed along with the appetizer plate and is immediately replaced by a dinner plate. In her book *Miss Manners' Basic Training: Eating*, etiquette expert Judith Martin points out how tricky this is to do. Since the diner is never to be without a plate in front of him, the process of removing one plate and replacing it with another must be executed with great skill. "This is done by having the server stand behind the diner, lean to the right to remove the service plate from that side, and then immediately lean to

the left to slip in the fresh plate." Yet another example of how good service is like a well-choreographed dance!

Service plates are not mandatory. Arthur Inch, the dining authority who served as an English butler throughout much of the twentieth century, never used service plates in his fifty years of service at great English estates. If you eschew service plates, use a dinner plate for the purpose instead, because, as etiquette expert Emily Post also reminds us, it is proper to always have a plate in front of the diner.

 DINNER PLATE

The dinner plate is usually between 10 and 11 inches in diameter and is set in the center of the place setting, about an inch from the edge of the table. If a service plate is used, the dinner plate is brought to the table after the appetizer dishes and the service plate have been cleared. Otherwise, the dinner plate is used as an underliner to the appetizer plates–Arthur Inch's preferred method. If this is the case, remove the appetizer dishes when they are finished, and leave the dinner plate in place for the main course. (If one of your guests has dripped something onto her dinner plate from her soup or appetizer, quickly substitute a clean plate!)

ORDER OF SERVICE

Whereas twenty courses or more might have been served at a Victorian dinner, today's formal dinner is a pared-down affair. Even so, quite a lot of food may be served. With a large number of courses, it helps to know what's coming, to limit consumption at the outset of the meal! A menu card is often placed on a formal table for this reason, to give the diner some advance warning.

A typical modern formal dinner may begin with a seafood appetizer followed by soup, or proceed directly to the soup. A fish course may precede the entrée. We think of the entrée as the main course, although the term once referred to smaller dishes served between the heavier courses. Vegetables were served as a separate course in the past, but today they are combined with the entrée.

The main course may be followed by salad, dessert, cheese, and fruit. Or salad may precede the main course, and the fruit or cheese course may be omitted. Each course is served with its own wine. Sherry may accompany the soup; white wine is served with fish and red wine with meat; champagne joins the dessert course. More complicated meals offer a greater selection of wines, including burgundy and claret.

Three of the above courses constitute most meals today, although a meal for a really important occasion can comprise as many as five courses. Remember Mother's warning, and save room for dessert!

It is quite acceptable for you to use a dinner plate as a main-course plate for other meals, such as luncheon, although a smaller salad or dessert plate can be used as a main-course plate for lighter meals.

 SALAD PLATE

The salad plate is 7½ to 8½ inches in diameter. For a European-style meal, in which the salad follows the entrée, the salad plate is placed in the center of the place setting after the dinner plate has been removed. For an American meal, in which the salad precedes the entrée, there are several options for where the salad plate is placed. If the host wants to have a salad plate on the table in the initial setting that also contains a bread and butter plate, he may place the salad plate either to the left of the forks (and to the left of the napkin if the napkin is there) or above the forks, moving the bread and butter plate slightly above and to the right of the salad plate (see page 61 for fork placement). Since having both a salad plate and a bread and butter plate makes for a crowded place setting, it is common to leave out one or the other at a formal dinner. If the salad plate is not in the initial setting, it is brought in and placed on top of the dinner plate when the salad course is served.

A crescent-shaped salad plate was often used in the Victorian era. You can still find this shape, which is meant to fit neatly with the dinner plate, above and to the left.

The salad plate has many other uses; you can easily adapt it to dessert, luncheon, breakfast, or tea. It can also be used for side dishes such as vegetables or as an underliner for a rim soup bowl (see page 32). Bernardaud, a French manufacturer of fine china, recommends that you purchase twice as many salad plates as dinner plates, since the salad plate is so versatile.

BREAD AND BUTTER PLATE

The bread and butter plate is usually between 6 and 6½ inches in diameter. It is typically placed above the fork, but its placement is affected by whether or not a salad plate is used in the initial place setting. This plate can do double duty as a dessert plate or as an underliner for iced desserts served in stemmed glasses and for iced beverages.

 ### DESSERT PLATE

The dessert plate is usually between 7¼ and 8½ inches in diameter, smaller than a salad plate and larger than a bread and butter plate. The dessert plate is brought out after the dinner plate has been removed and is placed in the center of the place setting (see page 118 for an example of a dessert setting).

Dessert plates can also be used for hors d'oeuvres at a cocktail party or for the main course at luncheon. In a typical five-piece place setting, the salad plate would double as a dessert plate.

 ### OTHER TYPES OF PLATES

A number of other plates were made in the nineteenth century for foods that were eaten frequently then but are less common today. You can find these plates in antique shops, and they add a touch of whimsy to your table. You don't have to use them for their original purpose, however. Examples of unusual antique plates include oyster plates, fruit plates, escargot plates, and bone plates. Asparagus plates were common because asparagus was usually served as a separate course. Since fish was often the first of many main courses, it had its own plate, about 9 inches across and easy to recognize because it was decorated with pictures of fish. Another plate no longer frequently made is the luncheon plate, which is a size smaller than the dinner plate. Today, a salad plate or a dessert plate can be used for luncheon, but an antique luncheon plate is perfect for serving cookies (and for luncheon of course, if you have enough of them!).

BOWLS

Before the use of flat ceramic plates became standard in the nineteenth century, all food was served in communal bowls. Bowls are used for more specific purposes today: to serve soup, fruit, puddings, cereal, or at more casual meals, pasta or stews.

SOUP BOWL

There are many styles and shapes of soup bowls to choose from, including:

rim and coupe soup bowl

cream soup bowl

- Rim soup: About 9½ inches in diameter with a flat rim about an inch wide, this shallow dish is more accurately called a rim soup plate.

- Coupe soup: Usually used in an informal setting, this rimless bowl can double as a cereal bowl.

- Cream soup: This two-handled bowl is set in its own saucer, which is a bit larger than the saucer of a teacup; it is suited to smaller portions of rich cream soup.

- Bouillon cup: A bouillon cup is often simply a teacup with an extra handle that is used for clear soups.

Most five-piece china settings include one bowl, the rim soup (some manufacturers call it a *rimmed* soup). It is proper to use the rim soup to serve all types of soup, pasta at an informal dinner, and cereal at breakfast. Limit your collection to the rim soup style, or add other shapes to suit your preference.

SOUP BOWL RULES If soup is being served as the only appetizer course, you may place the soup bowl on top of the service plate, so that it will be in place when guests are seated. The soup is then brought to the table in a covered soup tureen and served. An alternative is to bring soup bowls in after guests are seated, each filled and ready to be placed before the diner.

The soupspoon is the first spoon on the right side of the silverware setting. When you are eating the last of your soup, tilt the bowl away from yourself. If a soup bowl has two handles, it is proper to pick it up and drink directly from the bowl. After you are finished, leave the spoon in the bowl. If the soup bowl has its own underliner (for example, a cream soup or a bouillon cup, which are more commonly used at luncheon), leave the spoon on the underplate.

 FRUIT BOWL

This small (4 to 6 inches in diameter) bowl is used to serve fruit desserts and puddings, as well as vegetable side dishes. A salad plate or a dessert plate may be used as an underliner. If you are serving a fruit dessert, bring the fruit bowl and its underliner to the table when it is time for the dessert course.

CUPS

Most beverages at a formal meal are drunk from crystal vessels. The exceptions are hot beverages, which are served in china cups of various sizes and styles. Each has a handle and a saucer upon which it is placed.

 COFFEE CUP

The standard coffee cup holds 6 to 8 ounces and is used mostly at breakfast or lunch, when you want to drink more coffee. (Casual china sets often offer mugs instead of cups and saucers; these are good choices for breakfast or lunch but are not appropriate for dinner.) An after-dinner coffee cup is smaller, holding about 4 ounces, ideal for just a taste of coffee meant to act as a postmeal digestive aid. An after-dinner espresso is served in the

smallest coffee cup, a demitasse (also called an espresso cup); it holds as little as 2 to 3 ounces. If a place setting has only one cup and saucer, it may be used for coffee or tea and usually holds about 4 ounces.

COFFEE CUP RULES At dinner, the coffee cup is never part of the initial place setting. When it is time to serve coffee, the cups are brought in. The coffee may be poured either at the table from a china coffeepot (see page 42) or in the kitchen, in which case each cup is brought to the table already filled. Place the coffee cup before the diner with the handle to the right so that it is easy to pick up with the right hand.

 TEACUP

The teacup holds 6 to 8 ounces and is slightly shorter and wider than a coffee cup, to allow for quicker cooling. Bowing to the current desire for very large servings of hot beverages, many manufacturers of fine china make

both a teacup and a larger cup called a breakfast cup (which holds 11 to 12 ounces) or a mug to be used for imbibing a larger dose of morning caffeine. The French manufacturer Gien makes a teacup, a breakfast cup, *and* a low teacup (low tea is the proper name for afternoon tea). If you don't have these specialized cups, use the cup from your five-piece place setting, which holds about 4 ounces.

A *trembleuse* is a hard-to-find tea-service piece originally intended to be used by an elderly or ill person. The *trembleuse* consists of a large saucer with a small cuplike piece attached to it. The teacup is then fitted into this piece, which holds the cup steady if the drinker has shaky hands.

TEACUP RULES Tea is not commonly served at the end of a heavy formal dinner, as its flavor is too delicate, so teacups are most often used in an informal setting. Tea is a good choice to accompany breakfast or luncheon. Afternoon tea is also served, and the tea can be accompanied by a selection of snacks such as scones or finger sandwiches.

According to tea-etiquette expert Dorothea Johnson, it is absolutely *not done* to raise one's pinkie whilst sipping. Doing this in imitation of what one supposes to be fine manners will immediately expose one as *très gauche*. Ditto for wrapping the string around the tea bag to squeeze out the water, and sipping spilled tea from the saucer! The latter habit dates from earlier times when teacups did not have handles, and saucers were shaped more like bowls. Pouring the tea into the saucer to cool it saved the drinker's fingers from being scalded when trying to lift a hot cup.

If you take milk with your tea, the milk is typically put in after the tea is poured, so that you can see how strong the tea is first. In the film *Gosford Park,* the snooty lady of the house mocks a guest who pours tea for her by putting the milk into the teacup first. As Miss Manners points out, calling someone a "milk-first" type is an insult and an allusion to his lack of good grace.

CHINA SERVING PIECES

A variety of specialized porcelain serving pieces can be used throughout the meal. Some, like a butter dish or salt and pepper shakers, are placed on the table before the meal begins and left there through more than one course. Others are used only for the specific food for which they are meant; for example, you use a soup tureen to serve the soup.

Beautiful china serving pieces add a great deal to the look of your dinner table. Arrange them artfully on the table for visual appeal. Centuries ago, diligent hostesses drew maps before a dinner party, carefully noting where each serving piece should be placed on the table. This sort of advance planning is no longer necessary! Instead, place the biggest or most dramatic pieces in the center of the table and surround them with other large pieces like round or oval serving platters or bowls. Scatter the smaller pieces closer to the edges of the table. Be sure to keep things that belong together near each other: place the salad dressing near the salad bowl and the gravy boat near the meat platter. Arrange the food on the plate in an appealing and neat manner and always use the correct silver serving piece (see page 69) or an appropriate substitute.

Many china serving pieces come in standard shapes and are essential to dinner service. For example, it would be hard to serve a meal without a round or oval vegetable bowl and an oval serving platter, and both of these standard pieces can be adapted to serve any number of dishes. More specialized pieces like a soup tureen may not be necessary for your style of service or choice of menu.

Serving pieces are often made of porcelain, but you can also find them in silver, crystal, stoneware, or wood. You can complement your china service with accent serving pieces made of other materials. A typical bridal registry recommendation for the number and type of china serving pieces to have on hand includes three platters, two serving bowls, a gravy boat, a teapot, a coffeepot, a sugar bowl, and a creamer. A soup tureen is suggested as a nice addition as well, along with a cake stand and a covered vegetable dish.

SOUP TUREEN

soup tureen and covered vegetable dish

The origins of the soup tureen may lie in the large communal bowls once used to serve all foods. Perfected in seventeenth-century France, the tureen was made to be highly decorative as well as functional. The method of serving food *à la française* meant that all the dishes in each course were placed on the table at one time. In order to keep the food as warm as possible, the French developed serving pieces like the tureen with covers.

The soup tureen holds about 3 quarts and is one of the largest serving pieces on the table. Its many beautiful shapes and designs are a very dramatic and lovely complement to your table decor.

 SOUP TUREEN RULES

A soup tureen is necessary if you plan to serve soup at the table. If your initial place setting includes a soup bowl, then you will bring the soup to the table in a tureen, and serve it to each guest. Otherwise, soup bowls will be kept in the kitchen and filled there, then brought to the table; in this case, a soup tureen is not necessary. If you do elect to serve your soup in front of your guests, place the tureen either on the table or on a sideboard in the dining room. You will need a soup ladle to spoon the soup from the tureen into the bowls.

A soup tureen and a covered vegetable dish are similar in shape, although the former is usually larger (holding 3 quarts versus 2 quarts). You may want to own only one of these pieces and use it to serve both soup and vegetables (although probably not at the same meal, unless you want to wash dishes between courses). Use your tureen to serve other hot, souplike foods such as stew or chili.

COVERED VEGETABLE DISH

Like the soup tureen, the covered vegetable dish has a lid and is designed to keep food warm (see the photograph on page 37). Also called a covered casserole, it typically holds about 2 quarts. Most china patterns offer at least one style, whether oval or round. Because this piece keeps food warm longer, it's useful for buffet service. For dinner, it can be brought in with the other main-course side dishes and placed on the table. Guests should remove the cover when serving themselves. The cover should be replaced when everyone is done serving to keep the contents of the dish warm. If your covered vegetable dish looks presentable without its lid (i.e., it doesn't have a lip inside where the cover rests), you may use it without the cover as a substitute for a vegetable dish.

VEGETABLE DISH

This bowl is smaller than a covered vegetable dish and doesn't have a lid.

Most china patterns offer it in round or oval shapes. Use it to hold the dish for which it is named–vegetables–grain dishes, such as rice, or other hot or cold foods. Guests may pass this dish or other serving dishes to the person on their right.

OVAL SERVING PLATTER

The oval serving platter is a flat plate usually 14 to 17 inches long. Serving platters can also be round (often called chop plates). The French porcelain manufacturer Bernardaud recommends using a round serving platter for appetizers or cold main dishes, and an oval one for meat roasts, grilled fish, or poultry. If you don't have flat serving platters, you may substitute a dinner plate or a service plate, but it is handy to have at least one serving platter, since a place plate may be too small for serving purposes.

oval serving platter and round chop plate

GRAVY BOAT

The gravy boat, or sauce boat, will come in handy for any type of sauce served with the meal, or even for salad dressing. Often shaped almost like a genie's lantern, it is a long oval, with a handle at one end and a spout at the other (or, like the one pictured, with a spout at either end). It is always used with an underplate, which is sometimes attached.

Although a gravy boat has a spout for pouring, it is proper to use a gravy ladle to remove the sauce rather than pour the gravy directly from the spout. Using a ladle prevents the drips that inevitably fall from the spout and stain the tablecloth!

SALAD BOWL

Any large bowl will do for serving salad, but it is handy to have a separate bowl. This round dish is usually wider (more than 9 inches in diameter) and deeper than a round vegetable serving dish. Salad bowls are frequently made of porcelain, although they also can be wood. It is not typical to serve a salad already dressed, unless it is a Caesar salad. Serve the dressing in a separate serving piece, perhaps a gravy boat or a creamer. If you are serving your salad already plated, a salad bowl is not necessary.

BREAD TRAY

If you want to serve bread from a central serving piece, you can choose from many styles of bread trays: long rectangular servers, round dishes, and bowls. Some china patterns include dishes specifically meant to serve bread, but you can substitute others: a large bowl for rolls or a long narrow plate for a loaf or a baguette. (I recommend that you either pre-slice the bread for ease of service or include a serrated bread knife on the serving dish.) Or you can skip the serving tray and tuck a dinner roll into the pocket of a fancily folded napkin (like the ones on pages 112 and 118) or simply place it on a bread and butter plate before the meal begins.

BUTTER DISH

Butter can be served in a whole form, such as a stick or molded in a bowl, or it can be precut into pats or some other shape, such as balls or curls. It is served on a butter dish (or a small plate), and a butter knife is placed on the dish. The diner is expected to take a portion of butter from the serving dish using the butter knife, and place it on her own bread and butter plate. She then replaces the butter knife in the serving dish and spreads her butter on her bread using her own butter spreader. Don't butter the whole piece at once, and don't bite off pieces–it is proper to break off bread in bite-size pieces and butter one piece at a time.

A Salty History

Salt was once thought to possess great health benefits. To encourage the use of extreme amounts of salt, medieval and Renaissance dinner tables were set with huge salt cellars. These centerpieces made of precious metals held the life-giving (and pricey!) mineral, which was used in a liberal manner that would make modern doctors shiver with foreboding.

SALT AND PEPPER SHAKERS

Salt and pepper shakers are always placed on the table in a central location; use more than one set if you have a very large table. One small set can be placed between each two diners, to avoid passing them all around the table. On the Victorian table, salt was often placed before each guest in a small bowl called a caster, with its own tiny serving spoon.

Salt and pepper shakers can be made of porcelain, metal, crystal, wood, or some combination of any of these materials. Whatever you do, don't reach for salt or pepper, unless it is right nearby. Always ask for it to be passed to you. If you are doing the passing, always pass both shakers together, even if you have been asked for only one of them. If you can't tell them apart, remember that salt is finer than pepper, so its shaker is the one with more holes in the lid.

CAKE PLATE

The cake plate is round, about the size of a service plate, and has a handle on either side; its lovely shape is common in French china. Another common serving piece for cake is the footed cake stand. Cake plates can also be oblong. Some manufacturers make a three-tiered cake stand. If you don't have any of these pieces, any plate large enough to hold your cake will do.

COFFEEPOT

This large pot with a long graceful spout, a handle, and a lid is meant for pouring coffee at the table. Transfer the coffee you've made in the kitchen in your coffeemaker into this elegant server before bringing it to your guests. Coffeepots come in a variety of sizes and styles. If a line of china has two pots, the larger one is the coffeepot, and it often has straighter, more upright sides. If you don't own a coffee serving pot, it's perfectly acceptable to pour the coffee into the coffee cups out of sight in the kitchen and bring in the cups, two at a time, already filled. Don't serve coffee in a teapot, and do keep electric appliances out of the dining room! Serve coffee with milk or cream and sugar. (Most china coffeepots come with a matching creamer and sugar bowl.)

TEAPOT

Like the coffeepot, the teapot is meant for pouring a hot beverage at the table. A teapot is shorter and rounder than a coffeepot ("I'm a little teapot, short and stout . . ."). Unlike coffee, which is made in a coffee-maker and transferred to a coffeepot for service, tea is actually brewed in a teapot. This may be done with tea bags, but loose bulk tea is often preferred. If you use the latter, place a beautiful silver tea strainer over the teacup while pouring tea from the pot to keep loose leaves out of the cup.

If you don't use a teapot, pour tea in the kitchen. Pour boiling-hot water right from your kettle over the tea bag in the cup, and bring each guest's cup to the table already poured. Serve tea with milk or lemon and sugar on the side. Be sure to place a teaspoon on the saucer, and provide a tiny plate or bowl in which your guests can deposit their used tea bags.

clockwise from rear left: coffeepot, teapot, creamer, sugar bowl

SUGAR BOWL

The sugar bowl comes with or without a lid and holds any form of sugar: granular, cubed, brown, or white. (Vary the service silver to match the type of sugar, using a spoon for loose sugar and sugar tongs for cubes; see page 74.)

Guests should pass the creamer and the sugar bowl and sugar server counterclockwise around the table. Each guest should have not only an individual teaspoon for stirring his or her cream and sugar but also a saucer on which to rest the spoon. This rule applies to both hot and cold tea and coffee.

CREAMER

The creamer is a small pitcher with a handle and a spout that is used during dessert service to pour cream or milk into cups of coffee or tea. Creamers come in a range of sizes and hold from 5 to 9 ounces of liquid. The creamer and sugar bowl are usually a matching set. Your creamer also comes in handy for holding salad dressing or maple syrup at a pancake brunch.

OTHER SERVING PIECES

The following pieces are not essential for elegant table service, but you may enjoy collecting and using either new or antique versions to enhance your table: tart platters, relish or pickle dishes, egg cups, cheese trays, tiered cake plates with a silver stem handle, and fish platters.

CHAPTER 3

SILVER

THE BASIC FLATWARE PLACE SETTING

SILVER PLACE SETTING RULES
American versus Continental

TYPES OF PLACE SILVER

Knife
- *Dinner Knife*
- *Fish Knife*
- *Butter Spreader*

Other Types of Knives
KNIFE RULES

Fork
- *Dinner Fork*
- *Salad Fork*
- *Fish Fork*
- *Seafood Fork*

Dessert Fork
Ice Cream Fork
Other Types of Forks
FORK RULES

Spoon
- *Soupspoon*
  SOUPSPOON RULES
- *Dessertspoon*
- *Teaspoon*

Demitasse Spoon
Iced Tea Spoon
Other Types of Spoons

SILVER SERVING PIECES

Serving Spoon

Serving Fork

Carving Set

Shears

Salad Servers

Soup Ladle

Fish Servers

Butter Knife

Tongs

Sugar Spoon

Pie or Cake Server

Condiment Servers

If you are looking for the person with the power at any great English estate, seek out the underbutler–he's the one with the key to the silver vault! In fact, so awesome was this responsibility, according to English butler Arthur Inch, that the underbutler often made his bed in front of the vault and slept with the key under his pillow to prevent anyone from getting in!

Silver has been used for centuries to create beautiful items for the table, pieces that shimmer and glow with reflected light, creating a sense of magnificence as well as a show of wealth and power. Whereas only ten or twenty years ago, brides and grooms were shying away from purchasing silver in favor of lower-priced and lower-maintenance stainless-steel flatware, today newlyweds are once again eager to purchase the silver that they know will become an heirloom to pass on to future generations. Nothing matches the look of silver on your table, and nothing matches the feel of lifting up a weighty piece of silverware with which to dine in splendor.

THE BASIC FLATWARE PLACE SETTING

THE SILVER IN YOUR SILVERWARE

We often refer to utensils as silverware, whether or not they are actually made of silver. "Flatware" is a more accurate term that includes utensils made of any kind of metal or other material; in the United Kingdom the term "cutlery" is used. Almost all silver utensils are actually sterling silver (this excludes silver plate). Since 100 percent pure silver would be too soft for use, silver is always mixed with a small amount of an alloy metal to strengthen it. Sterling silver is mixed with copper at a ratio of 92.5 percent pure silver and 7.5 percent copper.

A standard contemporary American place setting includes five pieces: a dinner knife, two forks, and two spoons. The larger fork is a dinner fork; the smaller fork can be used for salad, dessert, or luncheon. The larger spoon is used for soup, the smaller one for tea and coffee. The knife is all-purpose. A traditional European setting contains four pieces: two forks (one large and one small), one knife, and a large spoon suitable for soup and dessert. (Many European manufacturers now also offer five-piece settings.) The four or five pieces in the modern flatware place setting are meant to serve every possible need, and they are all that remain from place settings common in the late nineteenth century that might have included as many as forty-two pieces.

Some diners prefer the American place setting, which includes a teaspoon, while others like the versatile place spoon included in a European setting. A host may choose to supplement the four- or five-piece place setting with extra pieces, such as a butter spreader, a fish fork and knife, a seafood cocktail fork, a steak knife, a demitasse spoon, an iced tea spoon, or extra dessert service forks and spoons. The usual recommendation is twelve place settings, with twelve each of any additional pieces likely to be frequently used, such as butter spreaders.

We have Herbert Hoover to thank for the limited number of pieces available in place setting and serving patterns, according to Victorian dining experts Wendell and Wes Schollander. As secretary of commerce in 1925, he encouraged American manufacturers to be more efficient and cut back on production. As a result, the number of place and serving pieces per pattern was reduced from well over a hundred to about fifty-five; today the number is closer to twenty.

SILVER PLACE SETTING RULES

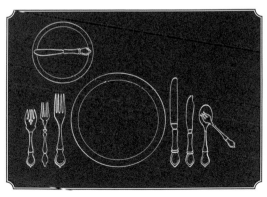

All silver should be evenly spaced about a half inch apart and parallel, with the bottom of the handles lined up in a straight line about an inch from the edge of the table. Forks go on the left, knives and spoons on the right.

If dessert silver is part of the place setting, put it above the plate. The dessert fork is closest to the plate and pointing to the right; the dessert spoon is above it and pointing left. When it is time for dessert, the guest will draw the dessert silver down on either side of the plate into its correct position.

A crucial rule: once you pick up a utensil, it should never touch the table again! When you put it down, place it on the plate, not on the table.

AMERICAN VERSUS CONTINENTAL

Customs differ in European countries. In America silver is placed faceup; in Europe, it is typical to place the silver facedown, forks with the tines down and spoons with the bowls down. When this custom developed, wealthy European hostesses sent their silver to the silversmith to have the insignia moved from one side to the other so that they would continue to be visible when placed down on the table.

Americans practice what etiquette doyenne Emily Post calls "zigzag eating." We cut our food with the fork in the left hand and the knife in the right, and then place the knife down on the plate and switch the fork to our right hand to eat. Through the course of a meal, the fork goes back and forth, from one hand to the other. Europeans eat in what is called "continental style." They keep their forks in their left hands and eat with them that way, tines facing down. It can be a challenge for the inexperienced to keep their peas from falling off the back of the fork before they reach their mouth. Either method is acceptable, just try to manage without dropping your food!

TYPES OF PLACE SILVER

KNIFE

The knife has been around longer than any other table implement, but it wasn't used for eating right away. Since everyone carried a knife around in the Middle Ages, it made sense to simply bring it along to

TABLE TEST

Q: What is the maximum number of any one utensil you will find at a formal place setting?

A: No more than three of any one utensil is appropriate. If additional pieces are needed, bring them in with the course with which they are to be used. (See page 60 for an exception to this rule!)

DECISIONS, DECISIONS . . .

Are you having a hard time deciding which flatware pieces are right for you? Imagine this: It's 1938, and you're reading an advertisement from one of the most respected manufacturers of silver plate, Wm Rogers Mfg Co. The banner at the top of the ad promises that the company is now offering you "A Thrilling Opportunity to Give Your Table the Perfect Setting It Deserves." All you need to do is select just the right pieces. And here are your choices—no problem, right?

asparagus fork
berry fork
cake fork (serving)
cold meat fork
dessert fork
dinner fork
fish fork (individual)
fish fork (serving)
fruit fork
ice cream fork
lettuce fork
oyster fork
pastry fork (individual)
pastry fork (serving)
pickle fork
salad fork (individual)
salad fork (serving)
sardine fork (serving)
butter knife (individual)
butter knife (serving)

cake knife, saw-back
    blade
dessert knife
dinner knife
fish knife (individual)
fish knife (serving)
fruit knife, hollow
    handle & solid handle
jelly knife (serving)
orange knife, hollow
    handle
pie knife
pudding knife (serving)
cream ladle
gravy ladle
mustard ladle
punch ladle
butter pick
nut pick
cheese scoop
cucumber server

tomato server
sugar shell
ice cream slicer
    (serving)
berry spoon
bonbon spoon
bouillon spoon
coffee spoon
cream soup spoon
demitasse spoon
5 o'clock tea spoon
ice cream spoon
iced tea spoon
long bowl soup spoon
olive spoon
orange/citrus spoon
salad spoon (serving)
salt spoon (individual)
tea spoon
sugar tongs

Source: Frances M. Bones and Lee Roy Fisher, *The Standard Encyclopedia of American Silverplate Flatware and Hollow Ware* (Paducah, Ky.: Collector Books, 1998).

dinner, and that was when the knife began its transition from tool and weapon to eating implement. The thoughtful medieval host would set up a whetstone outside the dining hall so that his guests could sharpen their knives before making their way to the table. This custom is the origin of the phrase "to whet one's appetite."

Did women also carry knives? Dining expert Margaret Visser thinks so: "Women must also have owned knives, but they have almost invariably been discouraged from being seen using them. . . . At many medieval dinner tables men and women ate in couples from a bowl shared between them, and when they did, men were expected courteously to serve their female partners, cutting portions of meat for them with their knives." Today everyone is responsible for cutting his or her own food, and a variety of knives has since been developed for different uses.

 DINNER KNIFE

The dinner knife is approximately 9½ inches long. You may also use what is called a place knife for dinner, which is slightly smaller (9¼ inches). A dinner knife is always necessary in a place setting for use with your main course.

 FISH KNIFE

If fish is on the menu, a fish knife may be found to the right of the dinner knife. Unlike other knives, the fish knife does not have a blade. It can be recognized by its distinctive curved shape. Its function is not to actually cut fish, which should be soft enough to cut with a fork, but to move sections of the fish to enable the fork to get at the flesh.

dinner knife

fish knife

butter spreader

butter spreader   *fruit knife*   *place knife*   *steak knife*   *dinner knife*

THE CARDINAL RULES

In seventeenth-century France, Cardinal Richelieu still found the concept of a knife at the dinner table to be threatening, and a law was passed that all table knives had to have blunt, rounded tips. Given his reputation for punishing dissenters, it's no wonder he worried about who had sharp knives at his table!

Today you'll see several styles of tips on silver knives, from the Richelieu-inspired blunt, rounded tips to a more pointed modern style.

Fish knives are made in solid silver as well as in silver with hollow handles and with sterling or stainless-steel blades. In the past, if a host or hostess did not have quite enough silver for the number of guests, he or she might give dinner forks and knives to the gentlemen, and fish knives and forks to the ladies.

Fish knives (and forks) are not essential. If you own them, they add a nice formal touch to the table setting. If you don't have them, a regular knife and fork will do just fine for eating fish.

 BUTTER SPREADER

At around 6½ inches, the butter spreader is the smallest piece in the knife category. No bread and butter plate should appear on the table without one if you are serving butter with your bread. Although the butter spreader is not part of the standard five-piece place setting, you will want to have one for each guest. If you don't have a butter spreader, don't serve butter!

 OTHER TYPES OF KNIVES

The Victorians, never ones to use the same item for more than one purpose, had a multitude of other types of knives: a dessert knife, a game knife (used to cut an individual bird, it disappeared by the early 1920s), a tea knife, and a fruit knife (which is still in use). Salad knives were also frequently used. Because the lemon and vinegar used to dress salads could tarnish or corrode many metals, a salad knife had to have a silver blade. The invention of stainless steel (first patented in the United States in 1911) solved this problem, and a separate salad knife was no longer needed.

Many of these alternative knives are not made anymore, although you can find and use antique versions. One other knife that is used today is the steak knife, which has a sharp, pointy blade. It was added to the table in the twentieth century and became more commonplace after World War II. Not all manufacturers make steak knives. If you don't have steak knives, use dinner knives or place knives, but keep chewy steaks off the menu.

KNIFE RULES The knife is placed directly to the right of the dinner plate. When setting the table, we place the knife with the blade facing toward the plate, even slightly tucked underneath, in a nod to its origin as a weapon. As noted earlier, Americans generally use their knives to cut their food,

*R*EVERE'S *W*ARES

The American silver industry started in the early colonial period. By far its most well-known silversmith is the famous patriot Paul Revere, whose work is found in museum collections.

*F*RANCIS *I*

Reed & Barton's Francis I pattern is featured in the photographs in this book. Designed by Ernest Mayer, it is the company's most popular pattern and celebrated its one-hundredth anniversary in 2006. Francis I is known for having fifteen design variations on the handles.

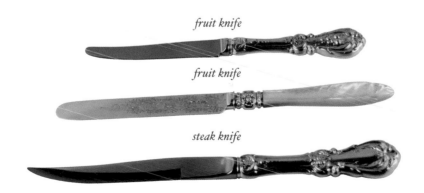

fruit knife

fruit knife

steak knife

then rest them on their plates while eating. Europeans generally hold their knives throughout the course. Either way, the knife never goes near the mouth! Long ago, when forks had only two tines and knives had wide blades, it was proper to eat food off a knife, but this is no longer the case!

TABLE TEST

Q: TRUE OR FALSE: You should use your individual butter knife to spread the butter onto your bread.

A: FALSE! This is my favorite trick question. The piece of silver that has been set on the individual bread and butter plate is not a butter knife. It is a butter *spreader*. The butter knife is the serving piece used with the main plate of butter.

FORK

It is common for people to project their anxiety about dining etiquette onto the fork. "How will I know which fork to use?" is the universal lament of diners concerned about embarrassing themselves at a fancy meal. (See "Fork Rules, on page 64, for tips!) For an implement that wasn't even commonly used until the mid–eighteenth century, it has certainly managed to generate a lot of anxiety!

The fork made some brief appearances early in the history of dining but wasn't embraced until the sixteenth century, when some upper-class Italians, sensing more sanitary methods of food consumption than using their fingers, began to use forks. Despite the support of these Italian trendsetters, fork use at the dinner table was slow to spread on the Continent and in the colonies. The utensil was thought to be too awkward and dangerous by the French, too feminine by the English, and too undemocratic by the Americans. Fork use did not

SEND A SIGNAL

You're at a fancy restaurant. You're in the midst of enjoying your entrée, but you set your knife and fork down for a moment because you're telling a really good story, one that requires hand gestures. Suddenly the waiter appears on your right and reaches in to remove your plate. Annoyed, you move to stop him, telling him firmly that you are not finished. "What a poorly trained waiter!" you think.

Is he really? Whose mistake is this?

A good server is trained to read a diner's signals; therefore, the diner needs some knowledge of dining rules and procedures. How do you let the server know when you have finished and it is time to remove your plate? When you are finished eating, lay your fork and knife diagonally across your plate, parallel and side by side, with the tips pointing to ten o'clock and the handles to four o'clock. If you need both hands to gesticulate, or would like to pause for a moment for the sake of your digestive system, place your fork and knife on the plate in an inverted V, with the tip of the knife pointing to ten o'clock, the tip of the fork pointing to two, and the two tips crossing. This is the "at rest" position. A good server will recognize your signals, and know when to take your plate and when to leave it.

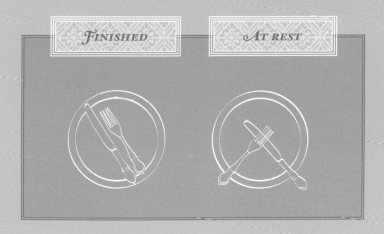

FINISHED   AT REST

become widespread until the mid–eighteenth century. Today, we eat with forks of many sizes, from dinner and salad size to the tiny seafood cocktail fork.

DINNER FORK

The largest individual fork, at 7½ to 7¾ inches, is the dinner fork, originally called the table fork. Used to eat the main course, including roasts, poultry, and game, it is found in both American and European place settings. Victorian place settings dedicated a separate fork to each type of main course, but modern ones do not. You may also use a dinner fork at luncheon.

SALAD FORK

Since salad forks have been popular for more than a hundred years, salad has long been featured on the menu, especially as improvements in refrigeration increased the availability of fresh vegetables. Part of the standard five-piece American place setting and the four-piece European setting, the salad fork is smaller than a dinner fork, approximately 6 inches. Americans typically serve the salad course before the entrée, so the

DON'T POLISH THAT!

Some salad silver is made with the additional protection of a gold wash. Gold is even more resistant than silver to acidic foods (such as vinegar or lemon used in salad dressings) and helps protect the forks. If you have silver with a gold or vermilion wash, be sure not to mistake this glimmer of gold for tarnish and try to rub it off!

TABLE TEST

Q: You should never place more than three of any type of utensil at a place setting. Is there an exception to this rule?

A: Yes. A place setting may have four forks if a seafood appetizer is being served. The tiny three-pronged seafood fork will be set on the *right* side of the place setting, often at an angle and resting in the bowl of the soupspoon. See the illustration on page 51.

*seafood
cocktail fork*   *salad fork*   *place fork*   *fish fork*   *dinner fork*

salad fork is set outside the dinner fork. Europeans serve salad at the end of the meal, so the salad fork is set inside the dinner fork, next to the plate. The choice is yours!

You may use a salad fork as a substitute for a main-course luncheon fork or a dessert fork. Fish forks or pie forks can be used as salad forks.

FISH FORK

The fish fork ranges from 7 to 7½ inches long, and is the only specialized main-course fork still commonly used. Its outer tines are thicker than the inner tines and are slightly curved to help them gently lift and separate the soft flesh of the fish. Fish forks come in both place (individual) and serving sizes. If you don't have fish forks, use dinner forks.

SEAFOOD FORK

Also called a cocktail fork, a seafood cocktail fork, or an oyster cocktail fork, this small (4½ to 5½ inches in length) appetizer fork has three prongs that usually curve toward the center, almost like a trident. If you don't have one, serve your seafood appetizer with a salad fork.

DESSERT FORK

ice cream fork ———

fruit fork ———

cake fork ———

berry fork ———

The dessert or pastry fork is usually about 6 inches long and has a bar connecting the tines. It can be placed above the plate in a place setting, or it can be brought in when dessert is served if there are already three other forks in the place setting. A pie fork, a subcategory of the dessert fork, often has a slightly thicker leftmost tine to help cut through the pie crust. Pie forks come in individual and serving sizes. You can substitute a salad fork for a dessert fork or a pie fork.

 ICE CREAM FORK

We might call an ice cream fork a "spork," a combination of a spoon and a fork, with a small bowl for a base and very short tines. Because ice cream was once made in large frozen blocks, a fork was needed to cut and eat it. Victorians, however, apparently enjoyed using forks any chance they had. Wendell and Wes Schollander, experts on Victorian dining, tell us: "One common joke was that the really fashionable people took everything but tea with a fork." If you don't have an ice cream fork, use a dessert spoon or a teaspoon.

 OTHER TYPES OF FORKS

berry forks

If you collect nineteenth-century silver, you undoubtedly have come across many types of specialized forks. If the food for which they were created is one in which we no longer indulge, adapt them to new uses! Antique silver is very durable, so there's no reason to keep it hidden in a drawer. With use, silver develops a lovely patina that only enhances its beauty.

Specialized forks include lettuce forks (which have three tines, large and splayed), baked potato forks (which have two tines, widely splayed), olive forks (which have extremely long handles and a small head with two or three tines), sardine forks (which have as many as seven very short tines on a wide handle), pickle forks (which look a lot like pie forks), and mango forks (very odd-looking three-tined pieces with a center tine that extends about twice as far as the other two). Victorian fruit forks, often called strawberry forks, are short (4½ to 6 inches) narrow forks, usually with three tines (not to be confused with lemon forks, which are the same size but have splayed tines). Strawberries were a novelty and very popular in the Victorian age, and a fruit fork was just right for rolling a berry in powdered sugar or dipping it in cream. These forks were originally sold in sets of six.

FORK RULES To avoid being tripped up by a fork, simply remember the following:

- Forks are placed to the left of the dinner plate (except for the seafood cocktail fork).
- When setting the table, place the forks in the order they will be used, with the first one to be used at the outside.
- When dining, always begin with the fork farthest to the left at your place setting.
- Move inward toward the plate with each subsequent course.

A HISTORICAL MELTDOWN

Many historians refer to the terrible time during Grover Cleveland's presidency when Mrs. Cleveland decided to melt down Dolley Madison's silver and have it made into a new design. People protested, and one manufacturer even offered to buy the silver from the White House in order to preserve it for its historical value. But Mrs. Cleveland ignored the outcry and proceeded with her plan, and the Madison silver was lost to history.

SPOON

Spoons, like knives, have been around for a while; they were the very first implement created specifically for the purpose of eating. The scooplike shape of the bowl occurs frequently in nature, and early spoons made use of natural objects like shells, often with wooden handles attached. Later spoons were made of many materials, including wood, metal, bone, and pottery.

Spoons were often given as gifts. The custom of giving an infant a spoon as a birth gift originated in the Middle Ages. From the late nineteenth century until about 1920, spoons with religious themes were greatly valued, such as Christmas or Apostle spoons, and commemorative spoons were also quite popular. A visitor then to Niagara Falls or Gettysburg would have brought home a spoon, not a T-shirt!

A standard American five-piece place setting has two spoons: a teaspoon and a larger spoon called either a soupspoon or a place spoon. This single large spoon has come to replace what was in Victorian times a multitude of options, including several types of soup and dessert spoons. With fewer spoons in today's place settings, the remaining spoons fill many functions. A place spoon works well for soup and dessert; a teaspoon is necessary for tea or coffee. Spoons are placed to the right of the dinner plate and to the right of the knife or knives (exceptions are indicated below).

 SOUPSPOON

bouillon spoon ———

cream soup spoon ———

place spoon ———

As there are many types of soup bowls, so are there many types of soupspoons to go with them. A long, oval-shaped soupspoon is meant for, as etiquette expert Gail Madison says, "soups with something in them," such as rice or vegetables, the sort of soup you would serve in a rim soup bowl. This spoon is the same size as a dessert spoon and you really only need one or the other.

A large round spoon is for cream soups. A slightly smaller round spoon with a slightly shorter handle is for bouillon, a clear broth served at the beginning of a meal. These other styles of soupspoon are not necessary to own, but if you inherited them from your grandmother, you should put them to use! In general, however, the large spoon provided with a four- or five-piece place setting will work well with any type of soup.

SOUPSPOON RULES When taking a sip of soup, fill your spoon only halfway, and run the spoon bottom over the edge of the bowl before lifting it to your mouth to prevent drips. Always move the spoon away from your body to take some soup. If it is a wide spoon for cream soups, turn the spoon and sip from the side. If it is an oval spoon, turn it toward you and sip from the tip.

If you are eating soup from a rim soup bowl, rest the spoon on the rim in between sips. When finished, leave the spoon in the bowl. If you are using a cream soup bowl, rest and leave the spoon on the saucer. Cream soups are usually served at luncheon rather than dinner.

🦐 DESSERT SPOON

Had you only one spoon at dinner, it would be this versatile spoon, which can correctly be used for dessert, soup, and cereal. Dessert spoons have the same shape as a teaspoon, and are halfway between a teaspoon and a tablespoon in size. They run about 7 inches in length.

Dessert spoons, if they are placed on the table rather than brought in with dessert, are placed above the dinner plate, along with the dessert fork. When the place has been cleared for dessert, the diner should slide the dessert fork and spoon down onto either side of the dessert plate (fork on the left, spoon on the right). Otherwise, the dessert silver is brought in on a plate and occasionally set before the diner with a finger bowl (see page 89). The guest removes the dessert fork and spoon from the plate and places them on the table in their proper location.

🦐 TEASPOON

This most basic spoon doesn't actually make its appearance on the table until dessert, when it comes in on the saucer of a cup of tea or coffee. It is useful also for other meals, such as breakfast or afternoon tea, for which it was originally developed to stir in cream and sugar and remove any wayward tea leaves. Teaspoons can be put to use for dessert as well. In a pinch, if you don't have a sugar spoon, a teaspoon can safely accompany your sugar bowl.

You may wish to buy extra teaspoons in your pattern–they do tend to disappear!

🦐 DEMITASSE SPOON

If your guests need a wake-up call after dinner, you might wish to serve a strong cup of espresso. The demitasse spoon is a miniature spoon used for espresso; a perfect match for those tiny cups in which this strong coffee is served. This spoon is brought in with the demitasse (or espresso) cup. You can also use these small spoons as condiment serving spoons.

demitasse spoon   teaspoon   bouillon spoon   cream soup spoon   iced tea spoon

place
spoon

melon
spoon

teaspoon

iced tea
spoon

demitasse spoons —

ICED TEA SPOON

This spoon has a bowl smaller than that of a regular teaspoon and a long
handle made to reach down to the bottom of a tall iced tea glass to stir
the sugar. At 7 to 10 inches, it is the longest individual spoon on the
table. In the American South, iced tea was routinely served with every
meal before the introduction of air-conditioning.

Whose Silver Was This?

Q: Why does the silver you inherited from your great-grandmother have her maiden initials on it, and not her married initials?

A: In the Victorian era, women were not allowed to own property. The exception to this
law was something called "paraphernalia," which included silver. Hence women engraved
the silver with their own initials, since it was one of the few things that actually belonged
to them and that they could pass on to their daughters.

Other spoons that might appear at a place setting include a citrus spoon, with a pointy narrow tip for digging out pieces of fruit; a salt spoon, with a round bowl and a 3-inch handle if individual salt dishes are used; a sauce spoon, which is rather flat and is used to scoop up the sauce from a plate and spoon it over fish or meat; a chocolate spoon, with a wide bowl; a parfait spoon, with a long handle; and an egg spoon. While some manufacturers still make new versions of these archival pieces, you are likely to find a bigger selection of unusual spoons in an antique shop. If you wish to add some spoons with quirky shapes to your collection, feel free to use them however you like (and have fun trying to identify their original use!).

citrus spoon

jelly server

berry spoon

salt spoons

ৡ𝐼LVER ৡ𝐸RVING 𝒫IECES

There are a number of common and essential serving pieces, both antique and new, that are frequently made of silver, and which will enhance your ability to serve in style. Various manufacturers recommend a combination of the following to ensure you have the essentials: serving spoon and fork (two or more of each), slotted serving spoon, salad servers, soup ladle, butter knife, cake/pie server, and sugar spoon. These will all come in handy for serving guests, or for guests to use to serve themselves.

SERVING SPOON

This large spoon, which may be twice the size of a tablespoon or even larger, is good for serving foods that can be easily scooped up and served with one utensil, including vegetables, rice, and other grains. It is often called a vegetable spoon, and is available in a pierced, or slotted, version that allows the juices or sauce to drain back into the serving bowl before placing the food on the plate.

*serving spoon and
pierced serving spoon*

SERVING FORK

Use this large fork for anything that it can neatly pick up and serve, including meats and vegetables.

The cold meat fork is a specific type of serving fork meant for sliced meat. One or both of its outside tines are thickened. If you have a cold meat fork, you may use it as a general serving fork for any type of dish.

*serving fork and
cold meat fork*

SILVER SERVICE

Victorians' creativity (and, apparently, their budgets) knew no limits. They applied their skills to silver serving pieces as well as place pieces, leaving antique collectors as well as those lucky folks who inherited their silver from Grandma with a wide range of fascinating shapes, from the sardine fork to asparagus tongs, some of which can be quite challenging to identify. I like to make a game of determining the original intended use of silver serving pieces, and offer you some samples to test your skills.

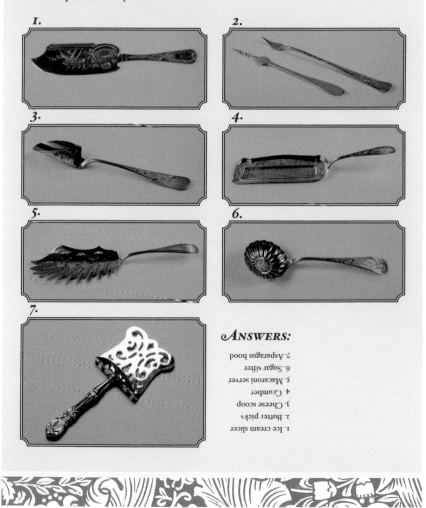

1.

2.

3.

4.

5.

6.

7.

ANSWERS:

7. Asparagus hood
6. Sugar sifter
5. Macaroni server
4. Cucumber
3. Cheese scoop
2. Butter picks
1. Ice cream slicer

EVEN MORE SILVER

There is a category of silver serving pieces that is often referred to as "hollow-ware," which refers to pieces that are hollow vessels, such as pitchers, jugs, bowls, teapots, and coffeepots. These large silver pieces are a wonderful addition to your collection, but are often quite expensive.

CARVING SET

In recent centuries, carving was an art that every hostess was expected to master. The carving set, including a long fork and knife, would be placed next to the hostess. When the game course was served, the bird would be brought in whole and placed by the hostess. She would carve each portion and place it on a plate, which would then be carried by the server to each guest. Today, game is usually carved out of sight in the kitchen, and only a few possess the talent for neat and precise carving! The carving set usually includes three pieces: the fork, the knife, and a "steel" for sharpening the knife.

SHEARS

game shears and grape shears

These dressed-up and decorative versions of scissors are used at the table mainly for two purposes. Game shears are used to cut game birds, and grape shears are used to cut off stems of grapes from the bunch. Although grape shears may seem quaint and old-fashioned, anyone who has tried to neatly wrest a portion of grapes from the bunch without the grapes coming off in the hand one at a time will appreciate this tool. Grape shears are small and delicate-looking, almost like children's scissors, since they need only snap a thin grapevine. Sharp and efficient game shears tend to be large and strong, since they must cut quickly through bones at awkward angles.

SALAD SERVERS

Salad servers work in a pair, as it would be difficult to pick up and serve salad with one utensil alone. They are generally made so that one resembles a spoon and the other a fork. Salad tongs also exist. If you don't have salad servers, use a serving fork and spoon for the purpose. Conversely, salad servers can often double as serving forks and spoons. Even salad tongs can be put to other uses: for example, to serve dinner rolls.

SOUP LADLE

This implement is used for ladling soup when it is served at the table. I recommend having at least one for soup and a second smaller one for sauces and gravies. A few popular ladles, in declining order of size, are a punch ladle, a gravy ladle, a cream or sauce ladle, and a mustard ladle. It isn't necessary to have all of them; for example, a gravy ladle and a cream ladle are close enough in size to be interchangeable.

FISH SERVERS

These are large versions of the individual fish fork and knife, the fork with its thickened outside tines, the knife with its distinctive curve. Use them for serving fish from the main platter. Fish servers are a lovely decorative addition to the table, but are not necessary items; other serving pieces—a pie server, for example—will work as well to serve fish.

BUTTER KNIFE

This piece accompanies the butter serving dish. Diners use it to take a portion of butter and place it on their bread and butter plate. They then use their individual butter spreaders to transfer the butter to their own piece of bread (observing proper etiquette by breaking off pieces of bread and buttering them one bite at a time!). If you don't have a butter knife, you may substitute a dinner knife.

TONGS

Tongs are a very popular style of serving piece, as they can be easily grasped and manipulated with one hand. Tongs are made in various sizes to be used for salad, ice, asparagus, and sugar.

SUGAR SPOON

There are many beautiful designs, both antique and contemporary, for this specialized serving piece, which is brought out with the dessert course and passed around with the sugar bowl. A sugar spoon, or sugar shell, often has a scalloped or fluted bowl. It is close in size to a teaspoon but has a slightly longer handle. Sugar is also served with tongs, when cubes are used. If you don't have a special sugar server, use a teaspoon.

Remember never to put the sugar spoon in your hot beverage—use your individual tea or coffee spoon for stirring!

PIE OR CAKE SERVER

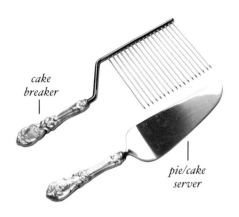

cake breaker

pie/cake server

This piece is shaped like a rounded triangle. The edge is used first to slice the pie or cake (some have one serrated edge), and then the piece is turned flat and used more like a spatula to lift the piece of pie or cake out of the dish and place it on the dessert plate. If you have only one dessert serving piece, this is probably the one to have. I find the pie or cake server is also useful for entrée dishes such as fish, casseroles, or lasagna.

*B*REAKING THE *C*AKE

One charming antique piece used for dessert is a cake breaker. It looks like a giant long-toothed comb with a long handle, and is used to gently separate slices of cake. It makes for a great conversation piece, as your guests will wonder what it is when they see it on the table!

CONDIMENT SERVERS

Pickled foods and condiments were common on the Victorian table. With refrigeration not readily available, meats and vegetables spoiled quickly. Pickled or marinated vegetables, such as olives and pickles, kept longer, and condiments like mustard disguised the flavor of meat that might not have been as fresh as one might have wished. As a result of these dining habits, a number of small serving pieces have come down to us that were meant just for these foods.

Olive forks and spoons have long handles and small heads or bowls, and the forks have two or three tines. The olive spoon sometimes has the center cut out, to fit the olive, and the fork has curved tines like a trident, for piercing and lifting an olive.

Many tiny ladles or spoons exist that were meant to scoop mustard or salt out of a dish (or caster, as it was called). Jelly and sauce spoons are flat with a curve on one side for slicing into the jelly and scooping up sauce.

Tomato and cucumber servers are round like big spoons, but flattened, with pointy tips. They are often pierced, to allow the juice to drip through. There are also smaller versions of these pierced spoons meant for bonbons, after-dinner snacks that were served in small bowls, or for nuts.

All of these serving pieces are relatively easy to find in antique shops, or you may have inherited some. Many silver manufacturers still make them today. While condiment servers are not going to seem as essential to your table as, say, a salad set or a vegetable spoon, they do add charm and style and are handy for many purposes. And, of course, if you haven't got a mustard ladle or a cucumber server, use a teaspoon, a serving spoon, or any of the other pieces described in this chapter!

TABLE TEST: THAT'S WHAT IT'S THERE FOR!

Q: Which of the following foods cannot be eaten with one's fingers at a formal dinner?

a. chicken legs   c. celery

b. asparagus   d. artichokes

A: Chicken legs. Use a knife and a fork to cut away as much meat as you can from the bone and then abandon ship. You are unlikely to see this casual food served at a formal dinner, however.

It is acceptable to pick up celery, or any vegetable served raw and sliced, with your fingers. You can also get away with hoisting a crisp stalk of steamed asparagus with your fingers, but feel free to use a knife and a fork to cut it, or even tiny asparagus tongs if they have been provided. Use your hands to tear off and eat artichoke leaves, but use a knife and a fork once you reach the heart.

CHAPTER 4

CRYSTAL

THE BASIC CRYSTAL PLACE SETTING
Crystal Rules

TYPES OF PLACE CRYSTAL STEMWARE

Water Goblet

Sherry Glass

Wineglass

White Wine

Red Wine

Champagne Glass

Cocktail Glass

Port Glass

Cordial Glass

Brandy Snifter

Other Types of Stemware

BARWARE

FINGER BOWL

CRYSTAL SERVING PIECES

Decanter

Carafe

Pitcher

Punch Bowl

Ice Bucket

The ancient Romans used glass, and historical evidence indicates that glass was created as long ago as 3500 BCE. In thirteenth-century Italy, being a glassmaker was an important profession. So valuable were the Venetian glassmaking secrets that the government forced all the glassmakers to live on the island of Murano, where authorities could prevent the artisans and the trade secrets they possessed from skipping town. In England, the formula for lead glass was perfected around 1676. Lead crystal was harder to manipulate than Venetian *cristallo,* but gave a more brilliant appearance, especially when cut. Lead crystal is distinguished by the lovely ringing sound it makes when tapped with a piece of silverware.

The late nineteenth and early twentieth century also brought great glass artistry, including works by Louis Comfort Tiffany (who exhibited his first collection in 1893), René Lalique, and companies such as the Swedish Orrefors (whose crystal is featured in the photographs in this book), Steuben (founded in Corning, New York, in 1903), and Swarovski. Crystal artistry is evident in a multitude of styles today, and the fragile beauty of crystal can be appreciated whenever the stemware on your table catches the light.

The Basic Crystal Place Setting

Most of the glassware found at the place setting falls into the category of "stemware," because it has–you guessed it!–a stem that connects the bowl of the glass to the foot. Other more cylindrical glassware for drinking may include tumblers (which can be used for water) or other barware (see page 88 for more on barware). The basic parts of a piece of stemware include the bowl, into which the liquid is poured; the stem, which is used to hold the glass; and the foot, the base upon which it rests. The bowl comes in a variety of

A Glass by Any Other Name . . .

As with Victorian silver, manufacturers went wild with style and shape once pressed glass was invented (in 1828). As described by antiques expert Sheila Chefetz, one pattern produced by the New England Glass Company included quite a selection: "ale glass, beer mug, bowls, candlesticks, Champagne glass, claret glass, cordial glass, custard glass, decanter, egg glass, finger bowl, goblet, ketchup bottle, lemonade glass, molasses jug, nappy [a small dish with two handles], pickle jar, spoon glass, sugar and creamer, and wineglass." They hoped, of course, that buyers would want them all!

shapes, from the round and full bowl of a balloon wineglass to the triangular shape of a champagne flute.

While it sometimes seems that there is a different glass for every type of alcoholic beverage (and there certainly are many types of glasses!), a traditional place setting will contain as many as, but no more than, five glasses: a water goblet, a red wine glass and a white wine glass, a champagne flute, and a sherry glass. The host may wish to have all of the glasses come from one matching set, or may decide to mix and match a number of styles and manufacturers. Either approach is acceptable, as long as the glassware is clear, clean, and streak- and spot-free (hand washing and drying immediately with a lint-free cloth is best) and arranged properly on the table. As for how many glasses you might need to own, American manufacturer Lenox recommends one dozen of each type of stem glass you plan to use, and eight of each bar glass.

CRYSTAL RULES

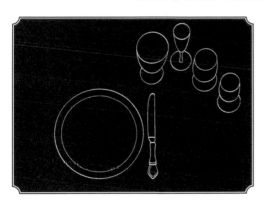

Place the water goblet above and near the tip of the knife. You can then arrange all the other stemware in the place setting in relation to the water goblet. You may arrange glasses in a row, with the water goblet at the far left, followed by champagne, red wine, white wine, and sherry. The sherry is to be drunk with the first course, the soup course. White wine is traditionally for the fish course (or for poultry), red for the meat, and champagne for dessert. If you are skipping a course or simply do not wish to serve a particular beverage, leave the corresponding glass out of the setting. However, if all five glasses are to be used, the row may look too long, so another setup can be used, such as a circle, a diamond, or a triangle. In this case, place the water goblet on the left, the champagne flute behind the goblet (as it is the last to be used), and the rest of the glasses to the right of these two.

The glasses are therefore arranged in the order in which they will be used, from right to left. This is for ease of use since, while food is served from the left, wine is served from the right. Be sure, when pouring, to fill wineglasses only about one third to one half full, to allow room for the wine in the glass to be swirled to enhance its bouquet.

Each glass is removed after the course in which it is used, while the water glass stays in place for the entire meal and is refilled as necessary. Typically, one would not refill any of the other glasses. A formal meal has a strict choreography, with each course assigned its own beverage. If a guest were to request seconds on a glass of wine, this would slow down the entire meal, since the plates and glasses for that course could not be cleared until this guest finished his second glass of wine. Hence it is proper to finish one's first glass of wine, and wait for the next wine to be served with the next course.

TYPES OF PLACE CRYSTAL STEMWARE

WATER GOBLET

The water goblet may be the largest glass on the table, with a capacity, when full, of 8 to 8½ ounces. In any line of crystal, the goblet represents the standard shape of the pattern upon which all of the other glasses in the line are variations. A water goblet can also be used to serve other iced beverages, although some manufacturers make a separate iced tea or iced beverage glass, which generally has a larger, taller bowl (holding about 13 ounces) and a shorter stem than a goblet. Be sure to refill your guests' water goblets when they empty them. You may also choose to serve water in tumblers, tall flat-bottomed glasses with no stems, for a more contemporary look.

SHERRY GLASS

Traditionally, sherry is served with the soup course. The sherry glass has a small bowl–holding 1 to 2 ounces–and is usually flared, like a trumpet. It is not always part of a contemporary place setting, because the wine is not served as regularly today as it was in Victorian times.

WINEGLASS

Wine is served at almost every formal dinner, and often more than one wine is served. For a less formal dinner, the host can set the table with just one generic wineglass, with a shape that will accommodate both red and white wine. This glass is often the same shape as the water goblet, but holds about one-third as much. However, if more than one wine is to be served, at least two wineglasses will be needed. Because your host will often be planning a new wine for each course, do not expect or request refills.

 WHITE WINE

A white wine glass is slightly smaller than a red wine glass, with a bowl that doesn't balloon out as much, because there is less need to aerate the bouquet of a white wine.

 RED WINE

A red wine glass is wider in shape with a larger bowl than a white wine glass. This extra size is needed to allow the drinker to swirl the wine in the glass to release the full aroma of the wine.

red wine glass and white wine glass

A traditional table of a century ago was set with two red wine glasses: a claret glass and a burgundy glass. The claret glass is the same shape as the water goblet and holds half as much. This is the glass we now use as the one red wine glass on the table. A burgundy glass—more common in France than in England or America—is larger than a claret glass and has a wider bowl to enable the wine to breathe. If you wish to match your wineglass with your wine, many fine manufacturers produce a range of glasses for specific wines, both red and white. Look for brands such as Riedel or Spiegelau.

CHAMPAGNE GLASS

The invention of the method for making champagne is often credited to the seventeenth-century monk Dom Pérignon, who is said to have called his confrères to partake of the discovery by saying: "Come quickly, brothers, I'm drinking stars." The treasured beverage first came about by accident when an unexpected second fermentation took place in a cask of French vin gris during shipping.

The most common shape for a champagne glass is the flute, a tall, tapered glass, almost like a trumpet standing on end, and holding about 6 ounces. A long-stemmed flute is preferable, so that your hand does not warm the drink. A tulip-shaped glass, one that narrows toward the rim, is also acceptable. Both serve the purpose of urging the bubbles up toward the rim of the glass and hence enhancing the aroma of the beverage.

The saucer-shaped coupe glass, said to be modeled on the shape of Marie Antoinette's breasts, fell out of favor after the 1950s, which will be appreciated by anyone who ever attempted to actually lift a full coupe glass from table to lips without sloshing its contents over the edge.

A champagne glass is part of the grouping of stemware on a traditionally set formal dinner table. It will be the farthest to the left next to the water goblet or in the back, as it is both the tallest glass and is used in the final course, when champagne is served with dessert.

COCKTAIL GLASS

Cocktails, or mixed drinks, have been imbibed since the nineteenth century. Cocktail glasses have shallow wide bowls, almost like the saucer-shaped coupe champagne glasses but with straighter sides, and hold about 2 ounces. Cocktails are usually served before dinner.

Some Bubbly Thoughts . . .

"Too much of anything is bad, but too much champagne is just right."

—Mark Twain

"Three be the things I shall never attain: envy, content, and sufficient champagne."

—Dorothy Parker

"Champagne is the only wine that leaves a woman beautiful after drinking it."

—Madame de Pompadour

"My only regret in life is that I did not drink more champagne."

—John Maynard Keynes

"In victory, you deserve champagne, in defeat, you need it."

—Napoleon Bonaparte

"I only drink champagne when I'm happy, and when I'm sad. Sometimes I drink it when I'm alone. When I have company, I consider it obligatory. I trifle with it if I am not hungry and drink it when I am. Otherwise I never touch it–unless I'm thirsty."

—Lily Bollinger

PORT GLASS

Shaped like a wineglass but smaller, the port glass is used to serve a potent after-dinner wine. Bring after-dinner glassware to the table when it is time to serve the port, cordials, or brandy.

CORDIAL GLASS

The cordial glass is the same shape as the water goblet but holds only 1 ounce. Cordials are very sweet after-dinner drinks.

BRANDY SNIFTER

The brandy snifter comes in a variety of sizes and consists of a deep bowl that is very wide at the bottom and tapers to a narrow top. It is shaped this way to capture the flavorful aroma of brandy, another after-dinner drink.

OTHER TYPES OF STEMWARE

Two popular drinks today are the martini and the margarita, both of which get much of their character from the glasses in which they are served. Both are on long stems and have a bowl shape that is basically triangular. The martini glass is straight-sided; the margarita glass has a distinctive curve inward just below the rim.

BARWARE

Barware consists of a wide range of glasses made for alcoholic beverages that aren't served in stemware. The most popular of these include highball (or tumbler) and lowball (or old-fashioned) glasses; beer mugs; and shot glasses. Barware usually isn't brought to the dinner table, but it is important to have barware on hand so that you can serve your guests' preferred drinks in the proper glasses!

GIMME A DOF, AND DON'T BE STINGY!

In some lines of barware, you may come across a dof glass, a name that stumped me the first time I encountered it. It looked just like a lowball, or "rocks," glass, used for a beverage drunk "on the rocks" (i.e., on ice). I soon discovered that "dof" stands for double old-fashioned. An old-fashioned glass is actually the correct name for a rocks glass; this one is twice as big!

FINGER BOWL

The unsophisticated dinner guest who drinks from the finger bowl is a film cliché. Contemporary formal dinners usually don't include the tradition of offering a bowl of scented water for guests to cleanse their fingers. A finger bowl may be brought to the table before a final fruit course or a dessert course; it is placed atop a doily on a small plate with the fruit or dessert silver on either side. If you are served a finger bowl, dunk your fingers and quickly wipe them on your napkin, then remove the dessert silver and place it on the table to the sides of the dish.

Whether sleek and modern in design or traditional and ornate, crystal serving pieces are a functional addition to the formal table. Most are used for holding and pouring beverages: decanters for wine and pitchers and jugs for water and other nonalcoholic drinks. You may have a crystal salad bowl or serving plate. And some of your serveware may be made from a mixture of crystal and some other material, such as salt and pepper shakers with crystal bodies and silver tops. Appreciate the beauty of crystal serving pieces on your table, and handle them with care lest they crack or break!

DECANTER

carafe and decanters

Before the cork was rediscovered in the seventeenth century, when wine was kept in barrels in the cellar, decanters were considered essential containers for alcoholic beverages. They were made in a range of sizes, including one with an eight-bottle capacity called the "Methuselah." One English manufacturer went so far as to make 606 different styles.

The decanter has a small flat lip for pouring and a glass stopper with an airtight fit. Today it is used primarily for red wine. To attain a fullness of flavor, red wine is decanted: it is poured out of its bottle and into a glass decanter so that its sediments can settle and it can breathe. Decanters are also used to hold liquors such as scotch and brandy. A decanter is not an essential serving piece unless you are a wine aficionado. If you pour wine for your guests from the bottle, do not leave the bottle on the table; put it out of sight on a sideboard or in the kitchen. Wine served from a decanter, however, may remain on the table. Because a full crystal decanter can be quite heavy, guests should let their host or the server do the pouring!

CARAFE

Unlike the decanter, the water carafe does not have a stopper. However, some modern crystal lines feature decanters without stoppers, so these two pieces can be used interchangeably. A carafe is a handy vessel for keeping a supply of drinking water or another nonalcoholic beverage on the table.

PITCHER

The pitcher was probably present in some form on the earliest tables. It comes in a wide range of shapes and can be made out of many materials. Use a pitcher as an alternative to a carafe to pour any type of non-alcoholic beverage. You may put cream, sauces, and dressings in a small pitcher instead of a gravy boat.

PUNCH BOWL

In centuries past, punch was served between courses during a large meal as a palate cleanser. Even sixty years ago, the punch bowl seemed like a much more necessary item, and was an essential gift for new brides in the 1950s. Today, the punch bowl and its accompanying ladle and cups are relegated to serving holiday eggnog.

ICE BUCKET

ice bucket

Because many mixed drinks and non alcoholic beverages require ice, it is handy to have a crystal ice bucket on a sideboard or in the bar area. Use tongs or an ice scoop to remove ice from the bucket and place it in drinking glasses; don't touch the ice with your fingers. If you don't use an ice bucket, bring each glass into the kitchen before you refill it and add ice directly from your freezer.

Top Ten Etiquette Errors

Most of us know the basics of good table manners. We say "please" and "thank you," we don't talk with our mouths full, and we try not to spill or break anything. There are a few things, however, that *some* people don't seem to know. Here is a list of my top ten terribly tacky things to do at the table. If you've been doing any of these things, cease and desist immediately!

1. ***Don't:*** Leave your napkin on the table until you actually need to use it.
   Do: Put your napkin on your lap as soon as you sit down. If it's a formal cloth dinner napkin, leave it folded in half on your lap, with the opening to the front.

2. ***Don't:*** Rearrange the table setting to make things more convenient for yourself.
   Do: Leave things as they have been placed, even if you see something you think is incorrect.

3. ***Don't:*** Eat before everyone is served.
   Do: Wait until everyone has food in front of him or her, unless you are at a formal dinner party and your hostess tells you to go ahead and eat so your food doesn't get cold.
   The corollary: If you are the last one to be served, and the delay is long, tell your dinner companions to go ahead and begin.

4. ***Don't:*** Reach across someone for something that is out of easy reach.
   Do: Ask for something to be passed to you if it's more than an arm's length away.

5. ***Don't:*** Pick up a utensil if you drop it on the floor.
   Do: Leave it there. Discreetly get your server's attention, and request a replacement. Do the same thing if you accidentally use your dinner fork for your salad and need a fresh dinner fork.

6. ***Don't:*** Butter a whole piece of bread at once.

   Do: Take some butter from the butter serving dish and place it next to your bread on your bread plate. When you wish to have some bread, break or tear off a piece and, using your butter spreader, butter only that bite.

7. ***Don't:*** Blow on hot food.

   Do: Be patient and wait for your food to cool.

8. ***Don't:*** Remove food from your mouth with your hand if you need to spit something out.

   Do: Put the unwanted bit on your fork and then onto your plate; try to cover it with some other food.

9. ***Don't:*** Leave your spoon in your coffee cup after you've added cream and sugar.

   Do: Place it on the saucer. The same goes for your iced tea spoon. If there's no saucer, try to find a paper napkin on which to rest your spoon.

10. ***Don't:*** Stack your plates when you're finished. Don't even move them out of the way. Don't touch them!

    Do: Wait for your server to take your plates. If you're in a restaurant and your server has let a dirty empty plate sit in front of you for an inordinately long time, get the attention of the next staff person you see, and ask for your plates to be cleared.

    The corollary: Don't start clearing plates until everyone has finished.

According to Victorian dining experts Wendell and Wes Schollander, things that used to be proper etiquette but no longer are include: drinking from your tea saucer, eating off your knife, using your tablecloth as a napkin, and gargling with your water. But one Victorian rule still very much applies: if something bothers you, keep it to yourself!

CHAPTER 5

TABLE DECOR

DECORATIVE TABLE ITEMS

Centerpieces

Candelabra

Place Cards

Bonbon Dishes

Napkin Rings

NAPKIN FOLDING

Sample Folds

Double Roll

Cardinal

Monogram

Goblet Fan

Ruffle Wrap

Corona

Bishop's Mitre

Artichoke

Stripes

Bird of Paradise

Since such an important aspect of a successful dinner party is the visual appeal of the table, it is no surprise that table decorations have always been an important part of table setting. From the most minimal (simple silver candelabra with white tapers) to the more elaborate (an epergne filled with fruit, place cards at every seat, elaborately folded napkins in the water goblets) each table has a personality, and this personality sets the tone for the dinner to be enjoyed there.

The style of serving dinner also has an impact upon table decor. Dinner was once served in a style called *à la française,* or in the French style. All the main-course dishes were brought out at once and placed on the table, and guests served themselves. In the late nineteenth century, people began to feel this service style made for a cluttered table, and a new style, *à la russe* (in the Russian style), came into vogue. Dishes were brought in one at a time, and guests did not serve themselves but instead were served either by a server or by the host. Once this new method took hold, it freed up a great deal of space on the table, which then began to be used for decorative items. The *à la russe* method remains popular today.

DECORATIVE TABLE ITEMS

CENTERPIECES

Once dining *à la russe* came into fashion, it became the norm to include centerpieces that were decorative rather than functional, such as flowers or a display of fruit. Prior to this change in style, a main dish such as a roast might have served as a centerpiece, perhaps raised up on a dish ring or a plateau–devices created for this purpose. Salt cellars, elaborately made of silver and other precious items, also frequently took center stage, as did the epergne, an elaborate dish with numerous branches to hold candles, fruit, or condiments.

The centerpiece should never be so high as to block sight lines from one guest to another. Don't let your centerpiece become overly elaborate. It should enhance the beauty of the table, not distract from it.

CANDELABRA

It is always elegant to dine by candlelight. A necessity at dinnertime in the days before electricity, candles are now used to create an ambience at once sophisticated and friendly.

A candelabrum is a candleholder with two or more branches, often made of silver. It raises candles to a height above the sight lines of the diners, and gives the table an imperial air. A traditional candelabrum would have as many as nine branches.

Candlesticks are also a fine way to include candles in a table setting. Beautiful decorative candlesticks are made in silver, crystal, porcelain, and other materials.

For a traditional setting, place two or three candelabra on the table, spaced regularly. This is compatible with having a floral centerpiece in the geometric center of the table. Candles on the table should be lighted before guests sit to dine. If you have a long table, consider using two or more sets of candlesticks.

PLACE CARDS

Place cards are a useful way to let everyone know where he or she is expected to sit for a small friendly gathering as well as for a larger, more formal get-together. Even if you don't have strong feelings about who sits where, draw up a plan anyway; this will speed up the process of seating your guests. If you decide not to use place cards, at least have in mind where you want your guests to sit, because they will ask where you want them to sit before doing so, and you should have an answer ready!

It used to be the custom that one would speak only to the guest to one's right for the first half of dinner, and then turn and converse only with the person on one's left for the second part of the meal. It's easy to see why dinner guests were quite interested in seating charts in those days, because a dull neighbor could really put a damper on dinner.

Position the place cards above the service or dinner plate or on the napkin or service plate. If there is a guest of honor, this person is traditionally seated to the hostess's right. The proper size for a place card is 2 inches by 3½ inches when unfolded. Fold this shape into a tent, and print the guest's name on the front. Proper form is to write the guest's title and last name.

BONBON DISHES

Small dishes with fruit or candy may be placed on the table before the meal and passed around with dessert (and served with a bonbon spoon). Dishes of nuts are traditionally removed after the entrée or salad course, whichever comes last.

NAPKIN RINGS

As mentioned on page 17, napkin rings were once used purely for practical reasons, to assure the ownership of the dirty linen! Today, however, napkin rings, while not essential on the table, are often used as decorative elements. They are made in a range of styles and materials, including metals such as silver and pewter, wood, fabric, and more. When setting your table with napkin rings, roll the napkin neatly, slide it into the ring, and place it across the service plate. When you are seated at the table, pick up the napkin, slide off the napkin ring and place it to the right of your place, and place your napkin properly (folded in half) on your lap. Your server will remove the napkin ring from the table. (See pages 104—110 for suggestions for napkin folds that work with napkin rings.)

Napkin Folding

The art of folding napkins into exotic shapes has a long history, although it has gone in and out of style. Seventeenth-century French kings had special napkin folders on their staff who created fantastic shapes for the royal family. It was considered a breach of propriety to actually use these napkins to wipe one's hands. The Victorians, being sanitation freaks, objected to the servant's hands touching the napkin any more than necessary, and hence for the most part eschewed fancy folds for plainer displays.

Napkins in earlier times were larger than they are today, with a standard dinner napkin being anywhere from 30 inches square to as many as 38 inches, as compared to today's 22 to 26 inches. Nonetheless, even with this smaller square of fabric, countless charming designs can be made to add a touch of style or whimsy to the table, and to complement the carefully arranged dishes, crystal, and silver.

Once folded, the napkin will enhance the look of your table, and it can now be called into service to hold things as well. Tuck a flower into a napkin fold, or a tiny package as a gift for the guest. The place card can be placed on or tucked into the napkin, and the napkin can even be used to hold a dinner roll.

As for where to place the folded napkin, the service plate is the most common place. Some folds do look nice tucked into a water goblet, and are especially meant for that. Some simple folds show themselves best simply placed right on the table, slightly to the left of the forks. Some folds are meant to stand upright, while others lay flat on a table or a plate, or get tucked into a napkin ring. For variety, try two different folds on the table at once, or use napkins in complementary but different colors or patterns. And keep in mind that a starched and slightly damp napkin is best for creating designs, and that the napkins you use must be perfect squares to achieve good results.

My suggestions for napkin folds to use at your table range from the simple and the traditional to the more elaborate. Some of the more complicated folds may require careful attention to the step-by-step instructions, but with practice you'll be turning out flawlessly folded napkins with ease. See how they enhance your table decor!

Double Roll

Even breakfast can be a special meal if you put a little thought into the place setting. Make sure your guests have everything they might need–a teaspoon for tea or coffee, a juice glass, perhaps an extra dish just for jam or butter–and set a simple but colorful and appealing table.

To maintain the uncluttered look, keep the napkin fold simple as well. The upright double roll fold is easy to do, and will perk up any breakfast table!

How to Fold the Double Roll

1. Start with the napkin fully open and flat. Begin at one corner and roll the napkin into a tight roll.

2. Hold the center of the roll in place with your finger and fold it exactly in half.

3. Stand the napkin roll upright in a water goblet or tumbler.

VARIATION

Use two napkins of different colors (both the same size) for the roll. To begin, place one open napkin over the other, with about an inch of the second napkin peeking out from underneath, so that they are slightly askew. Proceed with steps 1–3 above.

HOW TO FOLD THE DOUBLE ROLL

VARIATION

1.

1.

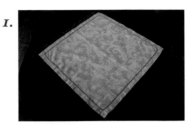

2.

2.

3.

3.

Cardinal

Brunch is a favorite meal for lazy weekend days or to mark special-occasion get-togethers. Include a large main-course plate to encourage indulging!

Tucked into a napkin ring and placed on the service plate, the cardinal adds just the right touch to a more casual meal.

How to Fold the Cardinal

1. Start with the napkin folded in quarters with the open corner facing away from you. (The "open corner" is the corner that has four loose tips.) Bring the bottom point up to about 2 inches below the top point.

2. Turn the napkin over, keeping the points facing away from you.

3. Take the top two layers of napkin and fold them down, with about 2 inches folded over the bottom edge of the napkin, forming a tail.

4. Fold the left point over about one-third of the way. Fold the right side one-third over as well, overlapping the folded left side.

5. Turn the napkin over and roll it so that it fits into a napkin ring.

VARIATION: CARDINAL SELF-BAND

1. Start with the napkin folded in quarters with the open corner facing toward you. Bring the top point over to the bottom points to form a triangle with a flat top edge.

2. Fold the bottom point up over the top edge, so that it looks like a hat.

3. Take the top two layers of napkin and fold them so they hang over the bottom edge, making a tail.

4. As in step 4 above, fold the left point over about one third of the way and overlap it with the right side also folded one third over.

5. Turn the napkin over. With this fold, you have created a self-banded fold, so the napkin ring is not necessary.

HOW TO FOLD THE CARDINAL

VARIATION: CARDINAL SELF-BAND

1.

2.

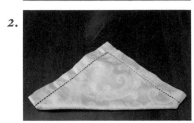

3.

4.

5.

1.

2.

3.

4.

5.

Monogram

A light lunch of soup and salad makes for appealing fare. Set your table taking your menu into account.

The monogram is a simple and straightforward fold, perfect if you have monogrammed linen.

How to Fold the Monogram

1. Fold the napkin in quarters, and place it so that the open corner (the corner with four loose tips) is facing away from you and you are looking at a diamond.

2. Fold about 2 inches of the bottom corners up.

3. Turn the napkin over and fold the left side in over the center line of the napkin.

4. Fold the right side in the same way over the just-folded left side.

5. Flip the napkin over.

HOW TO FOLD THE MONOGRAM

1.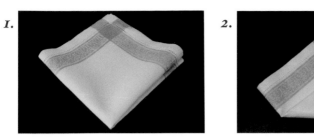

2.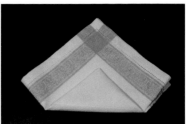

3.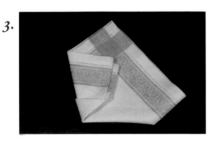

4.

5.

Goblet Fan

Luncheon is not as elaborate as dinner, but, even so, a fancy lunch may incorporate several courses, each with its own complement of tableware. Plan carefully and set an informal but proper luncheon table.

The fan fold is often seen on the service plate. Give it a new twist by tucking it into a water goblet.

How to Fold the Goblet Fan

1. Start with an open unfolded napkin. Fold it into narrow accordion pleats.

2. When it is completely folded, fold the narrow strip of napkin in half, making sure the edges meet evenly.

3. Tuck the folded edge into a water goblet, and fan out the folds of the napkin above the goblet.

HOW TO FOLD THE GOBLET FAN

1.

2.

3.

Ruffle Wrap

A traditional English tea is a nice way to offer your guests a simple repast with an elegant presentation. Tea requires many accessories, including a teapot, a strainer if you use bulk tea, a creamer, and a sugar bowl, plus cups and saucers, of course! For the sweets or finger sandwiches you may serve, use dessert plates or salad plates or even the smaller bread and butter plates. Make sure you provide teaspoons for stirring and knives for cutting pastries or forks if you serve cake.

Ruffle wrapped napkins are easy to place in a grouping on a tea table, so your guests can each take one as they are served.

How to Fold the Ruffle Wrap

1. Fold the napkin in quarters, and place it so that the open corner is facing toward you.

2. Starting at the bottom corner, fold the napkin in accordion pleats. (Note: unlike the goblet fan, the ruffle wrap calls for you to fold the napkin on the diagonal.)

3. Slip a napkin ring onto the center of the napkin.

HOW TO FOLD THE RUFFLE WRAP

1.
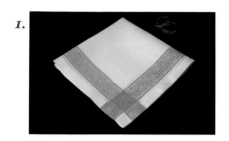

2.

3.
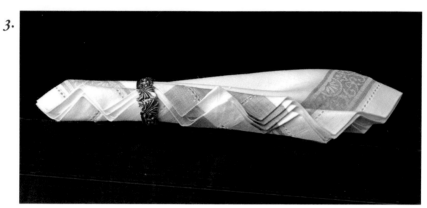

Corona

The semiformal table shown here utilizes a more casual style of china, with a mix of pieces, from the handcrafted square bread and butter plates and the pewter serving pieces to the African blanket used as a tablecloth. A consistent color scheme ties it all together. The overall effect is warm and welcoming, combining the proper with the unexpected.

The corona fold is not overly complicated, yet it has a properly fancy feel, making it just right for a semiformal dinner. Its array of points is reminiscent of the sun's corona.

How to Fold the Corona

1. Fold the napkin into a triangle with the point facing you.
2. Fold each of the two top corners down to the third point (this fold is call the shawl).
3. Fold each point on top up again, forming two peaks.
4. Take the bottom point and fold it up.
5. Fold the bottom edge up again, about an inch below the previous fold.
6. Tuck the points on the right and left underneath.

HOW TO FOLD THE CORONA

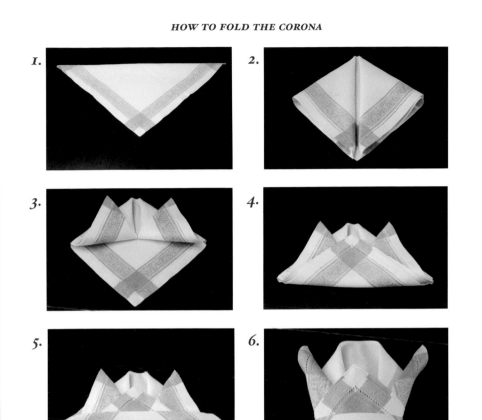

1.

2.

3.

4.

5.

6.

Bishop's Mitre

The formal dinner table shown here uses a simple, traditional china pattern for a very proper effect. You can't go wrong with this uncomplicated and elegant approach.

The bishop's mitre (or cap) is a very traditional design that is a favorite at great English estates–longtime butler Arthur Inch swears by this fold alone! It is a perfect complement for a table setting that makes use of simply elegant banded china.

How to Fold the Bishop's Mitre

1. Fold the napkin into a triangle with the point facing away from you.
2. Fold each of the two bottom corners up to the third point (the shawl).
3. Fold the bottom point up toward the top of the napkin, with the tip resting about an inch below the top corner of the napkin.
4. Fold this same point back down again, resting it about an inch above the bottom edge of the napkin.
5. Turn the napkin over. Fold the left corner over so it reaches just beyond the center of the napkin. Fold the right corner over this piece and tuck it into the first fold.
6. Stand the napkin up.

For variations on the bishop's mitre, you can fold the top corners out (some call this the lily) or tuck them into the bottom fold.

HOW TO FOLD THE BISHOP'S MITRE

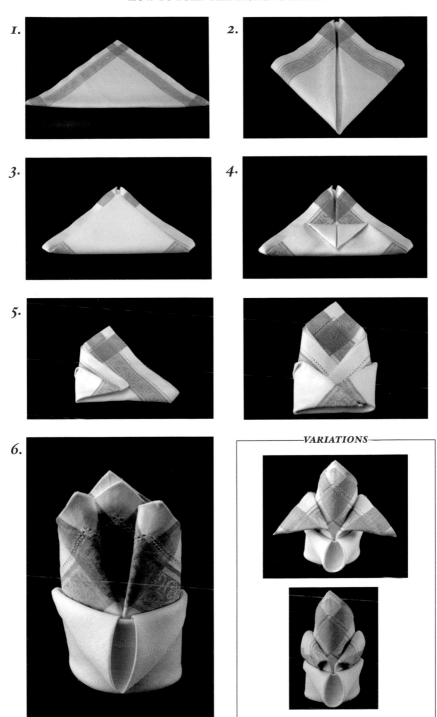

VARIATIONS

Artichoke

Don't feel constrained by the need to always have everything match! This formal table is artsy and elegant with its collection of mismatched antique French Limoges china. Even the crystal is mixed! The elegant cloth and matching napkins, along with the silver, help to pull the look together.

Just like the layers of leaves on an artichoke, the fancy artichoke fold creates elaborate layers of folded linen, giving your table a touch of whimsy perfect with the mismatched dishes. When it is finished, you might even wish to place the dinner roll in the center.

How to Fold the Artichoke

1. Start with an unfolded napkin. Fold each corner in to the center.

2. Once again, fold each corner in to the center.

3. Take the resulting square and carefully turn it over. At this point, I recommend you move to the service or dinner plate, because once this fold is complete, it is difficult to relocate it without mussing it. Now, once again, fold the corners in to the center.

4. Holding the points in the center in place with one hand (or use a tumbler or some other weight to hold the points in place), reach under each corner of the napkin and pull out the folded flaps from underneath. Tug gently on each corner to fluff up the design.

HOW TO FOLD THE ARTICHOKE

1.

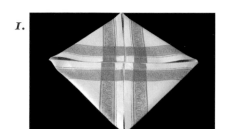

2.

3.

4.

Stripes

Coffee and dessert finish a dinner, or they can be served solo. Your guests will need the proper flatware for dessert–a small spoon and fork–and a cup and saucer for the hot beverage of their choice.

If you set a stripes fold on the service plate at a dinner, you might wish to tuck in a flower or place your dinner roll in its folds.

How to Fold Stripes

1. Fold the napkin in quarters, and place it with the open corner (the corner with four loose tips) at the top right.

2. Take the top flap from the top right, and roll it down toward the bottom left of the napkin, stopping about midway. Flatten the roll out with your hand.

3. Take the next flap from the upper right, fold it over, and tuck it under the first fold, creating a second band of equal width.

4. Take the next flap and do the same as in the previous step. You will now have three equal bands.

5. Fold the right and the left edges of the napkin underneath, leaving a rectangle with three bands running from upper left to lower right across the center of the napkin.

HOW TO FOLD STRIPES

1.

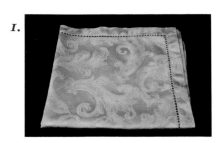

2.

3.

4.

5.

Bird of Paradise

Here's a traditional china pattern, simple but elegant, with silver and cut crystal–proper all the way! The fancy traditional napkin fold adds a graceful touch.

The bird of paradise is a dramatic Hawaiian flower, and you can re-create its distinctive shape with a napkin! This design works for any meal, but its folds are most dramatic when done with a large dinner napkin.

How to Fold the Bird of Paradise

1. Fold the napkin in quarters, and place it with the open corner facing away from you.

2. Fold into a triangle by folding the bottom corner up and under, so the loose corners remain on top.

3. Fold the right edge over, so that it creates a line down the center of the napkin. Fold the left edge over in the same manner.

4. Take the two bottom points and tuck them underneath, so you are left looking at a triangle with an opening down the center.

5. Fold the napkin in half by folding each side back. You now have an even smaller triangle with the opening on top.

6. Holding the tucked-in end in place, gently lift the layers of the napkin from the tip one at a time, pulling each one up to form the petals of the flower.

HOW TO FOLD THE BIRD OF PARADISE

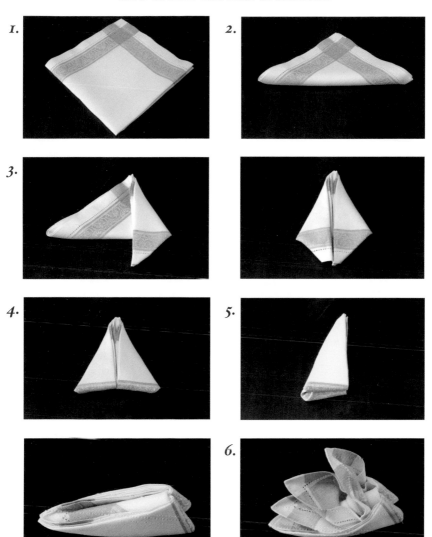

AFTERWORD: BON APPÉTIT!

I hope *Elements of the Table* will accompany you through many enjoyable dining experiences, and that it will help to make these festive occasions more comfortable and pleasant. Keep the book handy in your china cabinet, and refer to it whenever you have a question or need a refresher on the complicated rules of proper dining! With the help of the information in this book you will become not only a consummate hostess or host but also a guest who is always invited back!

BIBLIOGRAPHY

Belden, Louise Conway. *The Festive Tradition: Table Decoration and Desserts in America, 1650–1900*. New York: Winterthur/W. W. Norton, 1983.

Bones, Frances M., and Lee Roy Fisher. *The Standard Encyclopedia of American Silverplate Flatware and Hollow Ware*. Paducah, Ky.: Collector Books, 1998.

Bredehoft, Tom, and Neila Bredehoft. *Fifty Years of Collectible Glass 1920–1970*. Vol. 2. Iola, Wis.: Antique Trader Books, 2000.

Bryant, Chris, and Paige Gilchrist. *The New Book of Table Settings: Creative Ideas for the Way We Gather Today*. New York: Lark Books, 2000.

Chefetz, Sheila, and Alexandra Enders. *Antiques for the Table: A Complete Guide to Dining Room Accessories for Collecting and Entertaining*. Photographs by Joshua Greene. New York: Viking Studio Books, 1993.

DiNoto, Andrea, ed. *The Encyclopedia of Collectibles: Silhouettes to Swords*. Alexandria, Va.: Time-Life Books, 1980.

Dlugosch, Sharon. *Table Setting Guide*. New Brighton, Minn.: Brighton Publications, 1990.

Gaston, Mary Frank. *The Collector's Encyclopedia of Limoges Porcelain*. Paducah, Ky.: Collector Books, 1980.

Glanville, Philippa, ed. *Silver History & Design*. New York: Harry N. Abrams, 1997.

Hetzer, Linda. *The Simple Art of Napkin Folding: 94 Fancy Folds for Every Tabletop Occasion*. New York: William Morrow, 1980.

Inch, Arthur, and Arlene Hirst. *Dinner Is Served: An English Butler's Guide to the Art of the Table*. Philadelphia: Running Press, 2003.

Johnson, Dorothea. *Tea & Etiquette: Taking Tea for Business and Pleasure*. Washington, D.C.: Capital Books, 2000.

Kemp, Jim. *Stylish Settings: The Art of Tabletop Design*. New York: Gallery Books/W. H. Smith, 1986.

Lawrence, Elizabeth K. *The Lenox Book of Home Entertaining and Etiquette*. New York: Crown, 1989.

Loring, John, and Henry B. Platt. *The New Tiffany Table Settings.* Garden City, N.Y.: Doubleday, 1981.

Martin, Judith. *Miss Manners' Basic Training: Eating.* New York: Crown, 1997.

——. *Miss Manners' Guide to Excruciatingly Correct Behavior.* New York: W. W. Norton, 2005.

Osterberg, Richard. *Sterling Silver Flatware for Dining Elegance.* Rev. 2nd ed. Atglen, Pa.: Schiffer Publishing, 1999.

O'Sullivan, Joanne, and Terry Taylor. *The New Napkin Folding: Fresh Ideas for a Well-Dressed Table.* New York: Hearst Books, 2004.

Patterson, Jerry E. *Porcelain.* New York: Cooper-Hewitt Museum, 1979.

Post, Emily. *Emily Post's Advice for Every Dining Occasion.* Revised by Elizabeth L. Post. New York: HarperCollins, 1994.

Rinker, Harry L. *Dinnerware of the 20th Century: The Top 500 Patterns.* New York: House of Collectibles/Random House, 1997.

Savage, George. *Glass and Glassware.* London: Octopus Books, 1978.

Schollander, Wendell, and Wes Schollander. *Forgotten Elegance: The Art, Artifacts, and Peculiar History of Victorian and Edwardian Entertaining in America.* Westport, Conn.: Greenwood Press, 2002.

Spillman, Jane Shadel. *Glass Tableware, Bowls & Vases.* New York: Alfred A. Knopf, 1982.

Visser, Margaret. *The Rituals of Dinner: The Origins, Evolution, Eccentricities, and Meaning of Table Manners.* New York: Penguin, 1991.

Von Drachenfels, Suzanne. *The Art of the Table: A Complete Guide to Table Setting, Table Manners, and Tableware.* New York: Simon & Schuster, 2000.

Wolfman, Peri, and Charles Gold. *Forks, Knives & Spoons.* New York: Clarkson Potter, 1994.

——. *The Perfect Setting.* New York: Harry N. Abrams, 1985.

Zerwick, Chloe. *A Short History of Glass.* Corning, N.Y.: Corning Museum of Glass, 1980.

ACKNOWLEDGMENTS

First of all, endless thanks to my mother, Marcia Rosen, for forcing me to properly set all those tables for all those years, for sharing her love of fine china, crystal, and silver, and for hosting all the delicious meals that have been served on those dishes. And thanks galore to her cohost, my father, Walter Rosen, who took his turn behind the camera and created art. Thanks, Dad, for your vision and for your extraordinary patience and care for this project.

And to my husband and sons, Evan, Cooper, and Oren–thank you for sharing a table with me (almost) every night, and for having such lovely manners! And thank you for pretending not to notice that I am much better at setting a pretty table than I am at preparing the food to fill those plates! Thanks to my brother, Adam, who patiently listened while I babbled on about the history of forks.

To Patrick Snook, thank you so very very much for stepping in and adding your special artistry to the book's photography, and for sharing all those cups of tea with me. Bloody good of you!

Huge thanks to my editors, Maria Gagliano and Adrienne Jozwick, who are supportive, patient, and always interested in the subject, and whose thoughtful and detailed attention to my work has been extremely important to me. And to Pam Krauss of Clarkson Potter, who first appreciated and acquired my work; Marysarah Quinn, Laura Palese, and Danielle Deschenes, who have true vision; and Doris Cooper, who was supportive from the start. Thanks also to the ever-witty and well-read David Phethean for all the great chats over the years.

Thanks to the companies who have generously lent me their beautiful products for the photographs on these pages, and to the individuals there who made it happen: George Davis and Kim Madden of Reed & Barton, Tara Frazier at SFERRA Fine Linens, Cheryl Bruskin at Haviland-Limoges, and Valori Peterson and Robin Spink at Orrefors. Photographs in the book also feature pieces from the collections of Marcia Rosen and Lisa Deitch.

My thanks to various experts who kindly took the time to meet with me, show me around, and share from their vast stores of knowledge. I thank Darren Poupore of the Biltmore Estate in Asheville, North Carolina. At Replacements Ltd. in Greensboro, North Carolina, the place with every fork, plate, and teacup you could ever imagine or covet, I thank all the folks who took the time to help me, particularly Liam Sullivan, Chris Kirkman and the entire curator department, and Jan Couch and Sandy Lynch in silver. Thanks to Shirley Swaab, who invited me to give my first talk on the history of dining, and to Camille Focarino of the Philadelphia Museum of Art both for inviting me to speak and for her enthusiastic and ongoing support of my work. To Sunny Yi, then of Bloomingdale's, for her insights and tips, and to Sherry Berger for the great illustrations. Thanks to Robert Watson, butler extraordinaire, for looking the book over. And finally, I am grateful to Arthur Inch, a grand man with an instinct for elegance.